SAID ON OPERA

SAID ON OPERA

EDWARD W. SAID

Edited by Wouter Capitain
Foreword by Peter Sellars

Columbia University Press
New York

Columbia University Press
Publishers Since 1893
New York Chichester, West Sussex
cup.columbia.edu

Library of Congress Cataloging-in-Publication Data

Names: Said, Edward W., author. | Capitain, Wouter, 1985– editor. | Sellars, Peter, other.
Title: Said on opera / Edward W. Said; edited by Wouter Capitain; foreword by Peter Sellars.
Description: New York : Columbia University Press, 2023. | Includes bibliographical references and index.
Identifiers: LCCN 2023030684 (print) | LCCN 2023030685 (ebook) | ISBN 9780231212007 (hardback) | ISBN 9780231212014 (trade paperback) | ISBN 9780231559164 (ebook)
Subjects: LCSH: Mozart, Wolfgang Amadeus, 1756–1791. Così fan tutte. | Beethoven, Ludwig van, 1770–1827. Fidelio (1814) | Berlioz, Hector, 1803–1869. Troyens. | Wagner, Richard, 1813–1883. Meistersinger von Nürnberg. | Opera.
Classification: LCC ML1700 .S15 2023 (print) | LCC ML1700 (ebook) | DDC 782.1092/2—dc23/eng/20230630
LC record available at https://lccn.loc.gov/2023030684
LC ebook record available at https://lccn.loc.gov/2023030685

Printed and bound by CPI Group (UK) Ltd, Croydon, CR0 4YY

Cover design: Julia Kushnirsky
Cover image: © Marion Kalter. All rights reserved 2023 / Bridgeman Images

CONTENTS

EDWARD SAID'S INNER MUSIC

PETER SELLARS

IN A CONTENTIOUS and liberatory era that gave the world a generation of brilliant "public intellectuals," Edward Said was one of the most compelling, articulate, dazzling, difficult, idiosyncratic, and eloquent voices. Edward was the voice of the refugee, the exile, the displaced, the disowned, the disenfranchised, and the disappeared. He was also perfectly coiffed, elegantly dressed, well spoken, erudite, charming, handsome, distinguished, and irresistibly contentious.

His third book, *Orientalism*, arrived like a tidal wave in the zones of privilege of cultured intelligentsia worldwide. In challenging the very foundations of white supremacy, the assumptions of cultural superiority and the West's condescending gaze toward "the other"—weaker, decadent, ethnic, and aboriginal cultures of conquered peoples—Edward brought up short comfortable Western rhetorics of connoisseurship, reportage, and, finally, of equality and democracy. Ultimately, this sprawling, wide ranging, and fearless book, in its dark heart, rendered the term "Western" obsolete and introduced global elites, class agitators, and students to a planet of shared rights, responsibilities, and creativity without borders.

Edward's work launched new fields of perception and research across multiple disciplines, becoming a reference point for liberatory and progressive movements of international cooperation, recognition, and common purpose at a moment when global capitalism announced that everyone in the world was the same, but not equal. Edward's writing helped bring us closer to a planet where we are equal exactly because we are not, and will never be, the same. Humans, cultures, and destinies are irreplaceable and not interchangeable, and what is happening in one small corner of the world, whether in Vietnam, Palestine, or, in our era of climate change, the Pacific nation of Kiribati, will affect every person on the planet.

The arrival of each of Edward's books became important public events, and his public appearances became occasions. After his radicalization in the Arab defeat of 1967, when, as a prominent, visible, and established Palestinian exile, he took up the Palestinian cause in both his writing and his public activism, these public appearances required exceptional stamina. He and his family were subject to death threats, violence, and harassment. Watching this deeply cultured, refined, bespoke, virtuosic, and articulate intellectual be brutally, crudely hectored and attacked in a lecture hall was a sobering and instructive experience.

In his later years, after receiving his leukemia diagnosis and embarking on an ongoing regime of indefinite pain and sheer fortitude, moving in and out of hospitals, between and sometimes during his lecture tours, Edward shifted the focus of his writing. Late nights in hotel rooms on the road or in convalescence facilities, he began to write an autobiography, examining his own origins and looking deeply at his youth lived in the Arab world, with the startling and intense title *Out of Place*. Edward's book, which is painful and revelatory, describes first growing up in Jerusalem and then going into exile with his family at the age of twelve in the Nakba, the expulsion of Palestinians in 1948, ultimately arriving in Cairo and living rootlessly, facing new political, economic, and social realities. Most of the displacements experienced across his extended family and friends were mostly unmentioned and not discussed at home.

In the memoir, his father remains critical and distant, and we never really meet his sisters. But, at the end of his life, Edward writes about his mother with deep yearning and affection:

> My father came to represent a devastating combination of power and authority, rationalistic discipline, and repressed emotions; and all this, I later realized, has impinged on me my whole life, with some good, but also some inhibiting and even debilitating effects. As I have grown older I have found a balance between these effects, but from my childhood through my twenties I was very much controlled by him. With the help of my mother, he tried to create a world very much like a gigantic cocoon, into which I was introduced and maintained at, as I look back over it half a century later, exorbitant cost. What impresses me now is not that I survived it, but that by biding my time within his regime

I somehow managed to connect the strengths of his basic lessons to my own abilities, which he seemed unable to affect, perhaps even to reach. What also remained of him in me, unfortunately, was his relentless insistence on doing something useful, getting things done, "never giving up," more or less all the time. I have no concept of leisure or relaxation and, more particularly, no sense of cumulative achievement. Every day for me is like beginning a new term at school, with a vast and empty summer behind it, and an uncertain tomorrow before it. Over time "Edward" became a demanding taskmaster, registering lists of flaws and failures with as much energy as accumulated obligations and commitments, the two lists balancing and in a sense canceling each other. "Edward" still has to begin every day anew and by the end of it normally feels that very little has gone right.

My mother was certainly my closest and most intimate companion for the first twenty-five years of my life. Even now, I feel imprinted and guided by several of her long-standing perspectives and habits: a paralyzing anxiety about alternative courses of action; chronic, mostly self-inflicted sleeplessness; a deep-seated restlessness accompanied by an unending supply of mental and physical energy; a profound interest in music and language as well as in the aesthetics of appearance, style, and form; a perhaps overelaborate sense of the social world, its currents, delights, and potential for happiness and grief; and finally, a virtually unquenchable, incredibly various cultivation of loneliness as a form both of freedom and of affliction. Were my mother to have been only a simple refuge, or a kind of intermittent safe haven, from the day's passage I cannot tell what the results might have been. But she had the most deep-seated and unresolved ambivalence toward the world, and me, I have ever known. Despite our affinities, my mother required my love and devotion, and gave them back doubled and redoubled; but she also could turn them away quite suddenly, producing in me a metaphysical panic I can still experience with considerable unpleasantness and even terror. Between my mother's empowering, sunlike smile and her cold scowl or her sustained frowning dismissiveness, I existed as a child both fortunate and hopelessly miserable, neither completely one nor the other.

Edward Said, *Out of Place,* pp. 12–13

The man whom we all knew as the confident, assured, and dashing Edward Said grew up thinking of himself as hopelessly inadequate, a failure from the beginning, ungainly, stubborn, isolated, and ashamed. The window into some kind of truth, consolation, and well-being in these emotionally formative years was the Western tradition of classical music. Edward took up the piano (eventually studying with the mysterious and brilliant Ignace Tiegerman, a Polish exile and conservatory director) and poured himself into Mozart, Beethoven, and Chopin as a refuge, as his own home away from home. When he practiced the piano or gave little recitals, his mother showered him with praise, and many of the high points of his teenage years in Cairo were attending concerts of the Vienna Philharmonic or the Berlin Philharmonic with conductors Clemens Krauss and Wilhelm Furtwängler in the company of his mother, who also took him to the small opera seasons of touring Italian companies in Cairo opera house that had been constructed for the first performances of *Aida*. In these outings, Edward's joy and fervor were alive and complete.

I think these early, deeply emotional experiences might suggest why Edward was determined to write about music throughout the rest of his life. He never stopped playing the piano, and, for all of the demands on his time and books to read and lectures to give at the height of his career and fame, he continued to write about music. He would always insist that he wrote as an amateur on the subject. Turning to music drew Edward back to a place and a practice that fed his inner life, his inner self, the private person whom the world rarely glimpsed.

As he became more active in the Palestinian cause, Edward continued to write about and teach the Western canon, but gradually he inflected that writing with an abiding sense of missing histories, voices, and lives that thickened the plot and recast traditional Western narratives into a larger context, charged with new moral and spiritual complications. The double consciousness of being a Palestinian, for whom everything is struggle, disappointment, and invisibility, fed the necessity to write in ways that Edward began to acknowledge as "contrapuntal," with the acute awareness that the dissonance of the opposing voice renders the harmony richer and touches the heart more deeply.

Edward was sent to elite British schools, which would prepare him for a leadership role in the next generation of colonial administrators after the British departed from Egypt. The memoir is stunning for the tactile specificity with which he remembers every slight from every teacher, the names of all of his teachers and classmates, and the sense of relentless loneliness that still abides within him sixty years later.

Every day at school, Edward needed to challenge the stupid authority of the British educational system, which punished students for speaking their native languages of Arabic or French and insisted on inculcating the British history of imperialist glory and the "great books." Edward's voice, which was consistently repressed, developed an edge that became resistant and intransigent. He received top grades but was sequestered and punished as a troublemaker, and awards were withheld, an aura of disgrace surrounding this difficult young person.

As it turns out, Edward's entire education was at elite institutions; he went from Mount Hermon to Princeton to Harvard and then was a professor at Columbia for forty years. He was prepared from childhood for "greatness" and spent his life discussing "the great books." Going to the opera and to classical concerts was an extension of that zone of intellectual aristocracy and privilege, spaces where the best people (mostly men) all knew each other and, of course, could identify and speak definitely about the greatest performances of the great masterworks. Classical music was a place where musical discourse was shaped by men with a sense of their own invulnerability and well-worn, lived-in authority.

In music (and in much else), Edward's intellectual daystar became the writings of Theodor Adorno. While much of Adorno's writing on music evokes today the sharp, bitter taste of a certain Cold War acidity, rigidity, and aridity and a particularly Germanic impulse for closed statements and sweeping, severe judgment, Adorno's ferocious intelligence and unwavering resistance to the empty triumph of capitalism remains irresistible and largely irrefutable. Adorno's trenchant essays were lifelong catnip for Edward.

But the deeper astringency that informs Edward's writing about music and, even more importantly, his experience of music as a performer and as a listener, was his commitment to the Palestinian struggle. If you have spent the day, the week, the month, and the year opposing, with every cell in your body, the ratification and enactment of the Oslo Accords, which go through in spite of your opposition, and inaugurate an era of unprecedented Palestinian suffering and oppression, you come to Beethoven's Opus 110 Sonata ready for the heights and the depths, the heartbreak, the despair, and the unfathomable consolations, generosity, and relief of this music.

Of course, it's no surprise that Edward's musical heroes were Bach, Mozart, and Beethoven, who died without public acknowledgment of the depth of their genius. Bach put his *St. Matthew Passion* on the shelf above his desk after one deeply criticized and contentious performance and never performed it again in the last decades of his life; in his final years, he turned to writing music for people who had not yet been born. Mozart died thinking that his major operas were failures. His successful opera (*Figaro*) was removed from the Viennese court repertoire by censorship, and his unsuccessful operas (*Don Giovanni*, *Così fan tutte*) were emotionally and politically beyond the pale for his aristocratic public, rendering him unemployable at court.

Beethoven, facing increasing deafness and isolation, began to write his most profound music, which reached beyond the emotional, political, and musical structures of his era. I somewhat disagree with Adorno and his negatively tinged characterization of Beethoven's larger, late-in-life projects. I think of the *Missa Solemnis* as a work not of retreat, but of a visionary artist who urgently needs to reach beyond the church, beyond the theater, beyond the concert hall, beyond the opera house, and beyond representative and unrepresentative governments whose only solution for every human crisis is more war. Beethoven wrote the *Missa Solemnis* for a public institution that did not yet exist and for a public that had not yet been configured. Beethoven was writing for a public that, like himself, was exhausted and disgusted and damaged by war—people reaching, calling, for new structures that might permit human beings to gather, exchange together difficult feelings, histories, and memories, seek out new affinities and new relationships capable of elevating common purpose, common cause, and create and build true coalitions.

As Edward wrote about his great aunt, who tirelessly attempted to help refugee Palestinians arriving in Cairo in the 1940s, 1950s, and 1960s, using all licit and illicit means to feed, house, and care for families in acute loss and distress, "the Palestinian must work within the system as well as against it" because the existing structures are not yet what we need. The search for new social, political, personal, and, yes, musical structures that are flexible, responsive, healing, humane, transformational, open ended, nonhierarchical, life-giving, and life-sustaining is the project of Beethoven's late period. Beethoven was using every ounce of his remaining strength to imagine and forge new music and new musical structures capable of bearing the weight of the world and personal responsibility, opening a space of spiritual refuge, recovery, lightness, and regeneration.

In Beethoven's last piano sonatas, Opus 110 and Opus 111, written while he was struggling with the immensity of the *Missa Solemnis,* we move from music of deep heartbreak and inconsolable grief to little, unexpected openings, where the small germ of an idea opens into a fugue or a set of variations. The word "fugue" comes from the Latin "to fly": it is the music of exile, of people fleeing oppression and closed structures. It means, take an idea and run with it. In the course of the elaboration of that idea, add new voices. The resulting counterpoint and contradiction create a dense and astonishing reality that was not present or imaginable before. In his late years, Beethoven became obsessed with variations because they are the paths to permanently open structures. His technique demonstrated powerfully that you can take any idea that you're offered, no matter how minor, pathetic, trivial, and insubstantial and create a series of variations on that idea that offer renewal, profundity, delight, new vistas, and deep fulfillment. And that is our work on earth. We are engaged in transforming the inadequate and the insulting into the transcendent and the reimagined. In the case of both fugue and variations, Beethoven's modus operandi is the radical inclusion of new voices, the radical juxtaposition of opposing realities, and the shaping of larger truths by inviting all sides to work together. These are protodemocratic structures that understand that human abundance is generated within and through a community, and that tragedy demands repair. In the overwhelming sorrow of the Opus 110 Sonata, Beethoven marks the final, transformative movement, *adagio ma non troppo–Fuga.*

Allegro ma non troppo. Slow but not too slow. Tragedy exists to slow us down but, ultimately, to move us. Profoundly. Leading us to recognize thoughts and actions that we must stop. And then to move us forward. Not too slow means, don't be paralyzed by the grief but keep moving until the grief leads to something new and motivates change. *Fuga*: fly away. And then fast, but not too fast. In Opus 111, Beethoven marks the slow movement, *arietta. Adagio molto semplice e cantabile*: slow, simple, and singing.

Of course, in Edward's final years, he was obsessed with the late works of great artists. Some of these meditations now arrive to us in his posthumous book, *On Late Style.* Edward discusses several aspects of the word "late": lateness as defying resolution, lateness as being ahead of one's time, lateness as refusing to give in or give up. There is a particularly moving account of Jean Genet's intensifying intransigence as he engages the Arab world in his last years. First, in his epic play *Les Paravents (The Screens)*, Genet mercilessly exposes the hypocrisies, absurdities, and atrocities of both sides in the Algerian war. Scabrous, elegiac, and strangely flotational, Genet locates the second half of the play in the afterlife, where all of the participants who tried to destroy each other meet again and now have to figure out how to live together. Finally, in *Le captif amoureux* (*Prisoner of Love*), Genet engages the deepening debacle of Palestine with tenderness, rage, and despair. His absence of sentimentality and understanding of what it means to be criminalized for life touched a deep chord in Edward.

Before he left us, Edward was determined to finish a small book on opera. This is the book that you now hold in your hands. One of the complications of such a project is that the works themselves don't stay fixed, but, like all of music (and most of the arts, and much of politics), operas reveal new layers of memory, meaning, and emotion, new colors and different temperatures, as contexts shift and new circumstances present themselves. One of Edward's most brilliant excursions into writing about opera arrives midway through *Culture and Imperialism*, when he undertakes an anatomization of *Aida* and excavates the original process of creating the characters, the libretto, the scenery, and the music as a colonialist enterprise of shocking proportions. He doesn't say much about the music, but I'm sure that he, growing up in Cairo, had little patience for this opera and its falsification of histories, lives, and issues that are appallingly still underrepresented, unresolved, and falsified by various credited and discredited regimes today. The occasion for the commissioning of *Aida* was, famously, the opening of the Suez Canal, a moment of colonial self-congratulation that entailed the building of an entire opera house in which to premiere the work, launching an architectural Europeanization of one half of the city of Cairo, which was razed and rebuilt to more resemble Paris.

Verdi was a committed revolutionary, visionary composer. Nearly every one of Verdi's operas involves a political assassination in the name of resisting an occupying army—a tacit and well-understood metaphor for sustained resistance to the Austrian Army, which had rendered Italy an occupied territory in Verdi's lifetime. I must admit that *Aida* always struck me as music to open a shopping mall. Then, a few years ago, I went to Venezuela to see El Sistema "in action" and attended a concert where Claudio Abbado conducted seven hundred kids who had grown up in difficult, violent neighborhoods and knew the meaning of poverty. When they played the triumphal scene from *Aida,* fifty kids stood up, brandishing their trumpets, and blasted those fanfares with swing, syncopation, and a swagger, a defiance, an exhilaration, that announced to everyone that a new world was arriving, and that they were the liberators. We were all blown away, and I suddenly had to change my mind about *Aida* in a blazing new context.

Let's just say that a new generation is here who know their Frantz Fanon, either from the page or right through their skin, and they are ready to allow these pieces to speak in ways these pieces have never spoken before. Singers like Julia Bullock and Davóne Tines are prepared to both critique and liberate the cornerstones of the repertoire, and finally we are moving to a place unimaginable in Edward's lifetime: new operas will outnumber the old ones in future opera seasons.

The present book begins with Edward's essay on *Così fan tutte.* I can't help but think that Edward's decision to identify Don Alfonso as the principal character stems from deeply engrained memories of his father, whose cynical, disinterested, and masterful domination of family life proceeded from some unbearable combination of omniscience, dismissal, and impatience, across much of Edward's life. He was constantly presenting Edward with new tests, new challenges, that were uncomfortable, embarrassing, and "improving" at every turn. In *Così,* Mozart demonstrates that no human being's life can fit into a science experiment, and that the symmetries so beloved of the baroque, rococo, and Enlightenment periods have no place in the human realm. We all have different paths and unspoken, unrealized yearnings that will never match the schematic and mechanical structures we are forced into and socialized to accept. Edward rightly calls attention to the fact that Mozart wrote this opera not from a classical source but impelled from his own crisis with his wife, Constanze, who was at a country spa having an affair with one of his students. All of the charm and scintillation of the music cannot conceal the actual anguish and melancholy that move throughout the length of the piece. This opera, like every Mozart opera, is a gesture of reconciliation and healing. Edward was painfully aware that some divides are unreconcilable, where there will be no healing, no peace. Sometimes emotions and resentments run so deep that prospects for recovery and resolution seem impossible. As someone who spent the last years of his life insisting that Palestinians and Israelis recognize each other and each other's histories, Edward's response to Mozart's attempt at reconciliation is moving and sadly unsentimental: this music is best when it is played and acted with as much lightness as possible.

Beethoven's *Fidelio* occupied Edward's attention for years. He saw many versions of it and even participated in the shaping of one production. In the essay in this volume, Edward debates the eminent Sir John Eliot Gardiner, who maintains that Beethoven's first version, called *Leonore,* is the better opera because, musically and dramaturgically, the steps toward the liberation of the prisoners are more realistic and offer more dialogue, exchange, and participation by a range of characters. In Beethoven's final version, performed everywhere today, a voice of enlightenment from a higher power outside the prison walls sends word that the prisoners are to be released. The cells are opened, the prisoners emerge into sunlight, and a new era begins. There are no backroom negotiations, there is no process. Edward argues that this is the version he prefers; he would rather that liberation come as a transcendent act of sublime recognition and transformation, as he writes, like an episode from Bach's B Minor Mass—an unexpected moment of divine intervention. I find this unutterably moving coming from a man who lived his whole life waiting for the voice from outside and higher up, in this case the voice from the United States of America, that to this day has refused to declare that the cells should be opened, that the prisoners must be freed, and that Palestine must have self-determination. Only music can create this space of freedom. In Beethoven's music, the kingdom of heaven is within us. Each of us, and all of us.

I am always drawn to operas that have no continuous performance history, that were premiered under difficult circumstances, that disappeared and are waiting for their moment to reappear and participate in potentially redemptive new histories with new audiences. Berlioz's *Les Troyens* is one of those works that came into the world painfully and didn't quite make it. Regrettably, it was rediscovered in the 1950s and 1960s, in Edward's lifetime, at the wrong moment, when the opera world was obsessed with spectacle, prestige, and official behavior. *Les Troyens* was reconstituted in the twentieth century as an inflated French grand opera by Meyerbeer. The quicksilver music of Berlioz was rendered pompous and heavy, and the drama was treated with elephantine, self-regarding bourgeois middle seriousness. It was in that context that Edward experienced this wild and uncompromising work. Of course, the opera itself stimulated and electrified his keen musical senses. Edward loved the piece and wrote about it wonderfully, plunging into the historical layers with his usual avidity and acumen.

I am still waiting to hear and see a performance that understands that *Les Troyens* is every bit as radical and hallucinatory as the *Symphonie Fantastique*. Berlioz treats history as a series of fever dreams, acts of imagination, nightmares, absurdities, and missed opportunities. The music is by turns deceptive, comical, delirious, haunted, mysterious, blazing, intimate, and enveloping. Berlioz's treatment of history is wildly poetic and provocative, and his characters touch the imagined worlds that inhabit the hopes and histories of every age, and that are not to be. *Les Troyens* is laced with all the laudanum of Berlioz at his most unstable, rapturous, and sensual. As his brilliant autobiographies indicate, he was no fool, no dupe, but a dreamer, and his political antennae were alert and imaginative. I hope Edward's beautifully wrought essay inspires new views of this incomparable and misunderstood score.

Edward held Wagner's *Gesamtkunstwerk*, his culminating florescence in the history of synesthesia, music, and art, in the highest regard. Wagner invented new worlds, moved across disciplines, histories, mythologies, and art forms to create immense, immersive works of infinite possibilities, interpenetrating realities, and hypnotic intensity. All of his life, Edward remembered the first sound of Wagner that he heard: on his family's gramophone in Cairo, a 78 rpm of "Hagen's Watch" and "Hagen's Call" from *Götterdämmerung*. These are not perhaps the musical selections that would make you attracted to

Wagner for the rest of your life, but for Edward it was a sulfurous moment that he never forgot: the darkness and strangeness of these little excerpts penetrated deeply into his young psyche.

Edward's essay on *Die Meistersinger* is gentle and nuanced. He acknowledges that Wagner the man had a number of monstrous, mendacious, and opportunistic opinions, but contends that Wagner the artist did not, finally, create anti-Semitic art. In this conviction he had the agreement and solidarity of the conductor Daniel Barenboim, with whom he formed a profound friendship in the last years of his life. Daniel has been one of the great Wagner conductors of this or any era, and Edward attended many of his incandescent performances. The result of their friendship was the formation of the Barenboim-Said Akademie in Berlin, housed in the radical chamber music hall designed by Frank Gehry in the form of a cosmic egg. Edward's wife, Mariam, continues to participate in this bold project, which gathers young musicians from across the Arab and Israeli worlds and surrounds them with culture, complex histories, performance opportunities, and new friendships.

A new generation of artists, informed, empowered, and impatient, is arriving. For all of us, the opportunity of reading Edward again and anew calls him back from the grave. A spirit as restless and inquisitive as Edward's cannot remain buried. His voice is with us. His questions and his demands remain before us. Inside the heart of the cultural historian, philosopher, and critic, the political activist, the lightning rod, lurks the soul of a poet. Aristotle spoke of the difference between history and poetry: history is about what happened, and poetry is about what might happen.

Edward was deeply taken by the work of the philosopher John Berger and the photographer Jean Mohr, a multivocal, interdisciplinary collaboration that offered, in Berger's words, "another way of telling." Edward was inspired to create his own work in dialogue with Jean Mohr, a meditation on Palestine titled after the poem by Mahmoud Darwish "After the Last Sky." In Edward's prose and Mohr's photographs, there is no rhetoric; there are only people. Edward's writing is intimate, personal, flowing, and tender. The realities are harsh, and the humanity is real.

Perhaps, in the years after his death, we will be able to hear better Edward's inner music, the lives behind his lives, and the stories behind the stories that must be told. It is my hope that, one day, as we are calling Edward back to talk to us, to debate with us, here in this world, we might be able to show him some things that are now emerging that he did not live to see and that he did not live to hear. It is my hope that, one day, some of those things might give him pleasure.

INTRODUCTION

IN MAY 1997, Edward Said delivered four lectures at Cambridge University about "Authority and Transgression in Opera." Subsequently, he planned to rework the lecture typescripts for a book publication. In an interview recorded in late 1997, he thus stated that he had "written a book on opera," although at that time he had not yet revised the texts into a book manuscript.[1] In an interview recorded four years later, he again remarked that he "really must finish" this book, for which he still had "basically the introduction and the conclusion to write."[2] Unfortunately, this was not accomplished, probably due to a combination of his terminal leukemia and his incredibly intensive schedule of teaching at Columbia University, lecturing at universities around the world, and publishing countless articles, interviews, and books about Middle Eastern politics, U.S. foreign invasions, democracy, the history of the humanities, and music—to name just a few of the domains on which he regularly offered his critical commentary. Now, more than two and a half decades later, his book on opera is finally being published.

The typescripts of his Cambridge lectures on opera are preserved in the Edward W. Said Papers at Columbia University. This archive contains an extraordinary collection of Said's drafts and unpublished writings, together with his teaching notes, administration, and personal correspondence, all of which was donated to the university where he had worked for four decades. These documents offer incredible insight into Said's work and enable researchers to study the development of his influential ideas and publications. In this introduction, I describe the background and origin of his book on opera.

The main question in Said's Cambridge lectures and this book is how operatic performance, on the one hand, exerts a cultural power and authority, while, on the other hand, it can fulfill a subversive and transgressive function in society. The initial outline of the lectures, which he sent to Cambridge University in October 1996, conveys the general gist of his argument. According to this outline, "The basic theme is to start with the current renewed interest in opera as perhaps the last home of high style in the arts, as a mixture of massive authoritative presence (big opera houses, the star system, the sheer demands of putting on an opera with complicated sets, a big chorus and orchestra, etc.) and within the opera itself a constant pushing at, and playing with, and undermining of that authority with all sorts of devices musical and otherwise."[3]

Said develops this argument through an analysis of four well-known operas: Mozart's *Così fan tutte* (1790), Beethoven's *Fidelio* (1814), Berlioz's *Les Troyens* (1858), and Wagner's *Die*

Meistersinger von Nürnberg (1868). In four chapters, he questions how these operas negotiate the power structures in which they operate. In the first chapter, he considers the representation of individual agency and autonomy in *Così fan tutte*. In the chapter 2, he presents *Fidelio* as a fractured opera that reflects Beethoven's struggle when trying to combine words and music together in a for-him exceptional noninstrumental work. In the third chapter, Said argues that the driving force of *Les Troyens* is war and conquest against inferior others, thus giving this ancient story about the Trojan War a contemporary resonance within a nineteenth-century context of imperial expansion. Lastly, in chapter 4, he engages with debates about Wagner's deeply problematic legacy and tries to extend the pre-Holocaust German nationalist sentiment in *Die Meistersinger* to a more universal fear of the loss of tradition.

Said initially planned to deliver six lectures at Cambridge University and, accordingly, planned six chapters for this book. Due to health constraints, however, the number of lectures was curtailed to four, discarding an opening statement and a final lecture about Bizet's *Carmen* (1875). The introductory lecture, tentatively titled "The Presence of Opera," would have outlined his general argument about the sociopolitical dimensions of this art form, both in historical and contemporary terms. This argument was partly incorporated in the text about *Così fan tutte*. The envisioned sixth lecture, "The World of *Carmen*: Exoticism and Domesticity," would have analyzed this opera in terms of late nineteenth-century stereotypical representation of ethnicity, gender, and the intersection between the two. Attention to this relation between multiple forms of representation and power dynamics certainly would have been a valuable contribution to his work on music, in which the consideration of gender and feminist perspectives is largely lacking—even if he admired Susan McClary's pioneering work on this subject and had already written a short essay about music and feminism in 1987.[4]

In the outline of the lectures, Said explained that wanted to extend his interpretive methods from the domains of literature and history (for which he was primarily renowned) to opera. His analytical approach in this book indeed resembles that of his influential work on the entanglement between the arts, the humanities, and colonialism. This resemblance appears most strongly in his analysis of *Les Troyens* and its relation to nineteenth-century imperialism. This chapter may remind readers of his seminal essay on Verdi's *Aida*, although Said clearly adored Berlioz's grand opera, whereas he loathed Verdi's stereotypical representation of ancient Egypt.[5] On a more general level, in his close reading of the four operas he considers narrative features that speak both with and against the contextual power structures in which they operate—in the past as well as in the present—corresponding to his contrapuntal reading of the arts in *Culture and Imperialism*, even if his analysis of opera does not always address questions of cultural othering and inequality.[6] Moreover, since opera is a performing art form, one in which musical, dramatic, and visual representation intertwine, an analysis of this genre in particular can elucidate how historical themes resonate in contemporary society. Consequently, perhaps even more than his influential publications on literature and history, Said's analysis of opera addresses the responsibility of reinterpreting historical works and highlights the interdependence between the arts, representation, and their sociopolitical ramifications.

Even if a substantial part of each chapter in this book examines the genesis and historical context of the opera under consideration, Said also emphasizes that the operas can transgress their immediate contextual power structures, through which they can become relevant to today. In the first chapter about *Così fan tutte*, he thus criticizes traditional stagings that treat operas as if they are unrelated to "our own contemporary world of ideas and politics." He instead appreciates stagings that opt for a more universalizing approach to historical artworks, such as Wieland Wagner's rendition of *Die Meistersinger* in the 1950s, or that explicitly highlight contemporary resonances in these works, such as Peter Sellars's recontextualization of *Così fan tutte* in the 1980s. Regarding *Fidelio* and *Les Troyens*, it is worth mentioning that, during the late 1990s, Said tried to intervene in their performance practice directly. In May 1998, he collaborated with Daniel Barenboim on a semistaged *Fidelio* production in Chicago. For this performance, Said wrote a new spoken narration for the protagonist Leonore to make her struggle with power and freedom comprehensible to a contemporary English-speaking audience.[7] In that same year, he accepted an invitation from opera director Gerard Mortier to contribute to a *Les Troyens* production at the 2000 Salzburg Festival, although those plans seem to have been abandoned.[8] These activities underline once again that Said was not merely concerned with the authoritative historical presence of opera, but considered it first and foremost as a contemporary phenomenon.

The four Cambridge lectures about opera were presented at their Department of English, thus addressing a literary rather than musical audience. In personal correspondence with the department, when negotiating a topic for the lectures, Said assumed "that 'English' isn't too narrowly defined, since as a comparatist I tend to range over more literatures than English."[9] They replied that they were indeed "conceiving English studies in the broadest possible style," and he was encouraged to explore a topic that would "stimulate interest more widely, outside the English faculty."[10] However, they may not have anticipated a detailed analysis of four operas, none of which is English or chiefly interpreted in terms of a literary frame of reference, even if Said occasionally meets his audience by comparing the operas to nineteenth-century novels. Obviously, Said did not adhere to disciplinary boundaries.

The first chapter of this book opens with the remark that Said is not "a professional musicologist." He emphatically positioned himself as an outsider to this field, characterizing his work on music as that of an "amateur" without a "professional musicological reputation at stake," as he described it in his first monograph on music, *Musical Elaborations*.[11] This amateur status did not keep him from publishing many essays about music, and about opera in particular, most frequently in the New York–based weekly the *Nation* (for which he wrote twenty-eight articles about music between 1986 and 1998) as well as for the *London Review of Books*, the *Observer*, *Grand Street*, and several other magazines and journals.[12] Strictly speaking, however, he never published a musicological article. Prominent journals in the field regularly inquired whether he would send them a contribution—including the *Cambridge Opera Journal*, the *Journal of the American Musicological Society*, and the *Journal of Musicological Research*—but he did not comply with these requests.[13] Documents in the Edward W. Said Papers nevertheless testify to a committed engagement with the discipline that mainly took place behind the scenes of his professional activities. For instance, he frequently corresponded with prominent musicologists such as Maynard Solomon and Donald Mitchell about his and their work in progress, he supported upcoming and progressively minded music scholars with letters of recommendation and similar means, and he tried to publish musicological books in his series for Harvard University Press.[14] Indeed, as he observed in *Musical Elaborations*, being an amateur is "not so disabling a status as one might think."[15] But whereas in *Musical Elaborations* this outsider status is used in order to criticize musicology, especially for its failure to connect historical and analytical inquiry to ideology and politics, this book on opera is more firmly positioned within this discipline, building upon and responding to its ongoing debates.

Although Said would not describe himself as a musicologist, the contents of his Cambridge lectures initially developed against a musicological background. In the spring semester of 1995, Said gave a graduate seminar on Opera and Society at Columbia University's Department of Music—the only musicological course that he taught in his career. The course description and Said's notebook indicate that the scope and contents of this seminar closely resemble that of the Cambridge lectures from two years later.[16] In the seminar, they discussed seven operas in detail: *Così fan tutte, Fidelio*, and *Les Troyens*, together with Wagner's *Die Walküre*, Verdi's *Aida*, Bizet's *Carmen*, and Strauss's *Capriccio*. The selected readings combined musicological literature by Susan McClary, Carolyn Abbate, and Jane Fulcher, among others, with canonical authors from other fields, including Nietzsche, Adorno, and Foucault. The classes covered a number of topical issues in opera studies, such as the representation of national identity, gender, and exoticism, and considered these both in terms of the operas' historical contexts and in relation to contemporary concerns. Yet, as Said remarked in his notebook, the contemporaneity of the operatic world is "hardest to grasp," because many opera houses are "most conservative art institutions" that behave like museums by trying to preserve operas as historical objects.[17] The course would therefore explore recent tendencies in performance practice and scholarship that challenge this conservative approach to opera—a concern that he would subsequently elaborate in his Cambridge lectures.

The musicological backdrop of Said's ideas about operatic performance clearly surfaces in his four lectures. Each offers a close reading of the opera under consideration, devoting attention to its puzzling characters, narrative ambivalences, musical peculiarities, and the like, meanwhile relating these characteristics to the social context of the composition and performance. These analyses sometimes include remarks about musical-theoretical details and encompass an extensive frame of reference with regard to composers, memorable performances and performers, prominent music scholars, and opera plots. This musicological frame of references, combined with the virtuosity of Said's prose, undoubtedly must have challenged a literary audience during an oral presentation. The written format of this book should make his insights about opera more accessible to an interdisciplinary readership.

The arguments in this book are obviously positioned in a mid-1990s context, mainly in the United States and specifically in New York, both with regard to operatic performance practice and academic debates. This becomes clear, for instance, when Said complains about traditional stagings at New York's Metropolitan Opera that eschew the contemporary resonances in these works. At the time that he wrote this book, however, other opera houses did adopt alternative approaches, both in the United States and in Europe, and since that time the Metropolitan Opera has gradually deviated from its conventional style by staging more abstract productions, performing more recent works, and finding audiovisual means to reach new audiences. Regarding academic debates, Said often responds to then-recent publications about the operas—for instance, when he considers the covert anti-Semitism in *Die Meistersinger* that was fiercely debated during the 1990s. More generally, he engages with a type of sociopolitical inquiry into opera that at that time was just relatively recently gaining proper musicological attention. Consequently, some of his critical remarks about operatic performance and academic debates may seem somewhat dated. Nevertheless, I believe that most of his arguments about these four operas, as well as about the genre in general, reach far beyond the specific context in which he wrote this text. To paraphrase Said, this book can be read both as an authoritative statement from a prominent late twentieth-century intellectual and as a text that may transgress its immediate contextual associations.

The four lectures were written as fully fledged essays, and it seems that Said intended to publish them as such. Indeed, in the late 1990s the first two lectures were published as articles in largely identical form.[18] His typescripts only required basic editorial revision for this book publication. I corrected the quotations in his text and added literature references. In most cases I could use Said's own annotated copies and editions of this literature from his personal library, which was donated to Columbia University. Regarding specific opera stagings that are mentioned, I sometimes clarified the year, director, or location, and in a few instances I deleted brief references to specific events in the 1990s. When necessary, I corrected the names of authors, composers, directors, and opera characters, and I corrected typographical errors in the lectures typescripts by comparing them to Said's handwritten drafts. In addition, I sometimes changed the interpunction to enhance consistency and readability, although I have been careful not to interrupt the flow and energy of his text. In the two cases where the chapters were previously published as articles in the 1990s, I usually followed the formulations in the lecture typescripts rather than in the slightly shortened articles, except when the published versions provide more clarity. During each lecture, Said played music fragments when discussing specific scenes in the operas. Although these fragments certainly would have enriched his talks, I believe that his arguments are clear and convincing without the musical illustrations, which nowadays can be consulted through online resources. When necessary, I specified the scenes to which Said refers.

The publication of this book was made possible thanks to the efforts and support of Mariam Said, Jennifer Crewe, and Jacqueline Ko. The research required to edit Said's texts was enabled by an Edward W. Said Fellowship from Columbia University. Parts of this book were previously published as articles during the 1990s. Chapter 1 originally appeared in slightly different form in *Grand Street*, no. 62 (1997), published by Jean Stein. Chapter 2 originally appeared in slightly different form in the *London Review of Books* (October 30, 1997). Sections from chapters 1 and 2 also appeared together in *Profession* (1998), published by the Modern Language Association of America. Sections from chapter 3 originally appeared in the *Nation* (June 27, 1994). I am grateful for the permission by *Grand Street*, *London Review of Books*, *Profession*, and the *Nation* to republish these texts.

SAID ON OPERA

Chapter One

COSÌ FAN TUTTE AT THE LIMITS

MOZART'S *COSÌ FAN TUTTE* (1790) was the first opera I saw when I first came to the United States as a schoolboy in the early 1950s. The Metropolitan Opera production was directed by renowned theater figure Alfred Lunt and, as I recall, much celebrated as a brilliant yet faithful English-language rendition of a sparkling, beautiful, elegant opera that boasted an excellent cast (John Brownlee as Don Alfonso, Eleanor Steber and Blanche Thebom as the two sisters, Richard Tucker and Frank Guarrera as the young men, Patrice Munsel as Despina) and a fastidiously executed conception as an eighteenth-century court comedy. I remember a lot of curtseying, many lace hankies, elaborate wigs, and acres of beauty spots, much chuckling and all-around good fun, all of which seemed to go well with the very polished—indeed, even superb—singing by the ensemble. So powerful was the impression made on me by this *Così fan tutte* that most of the many subsequent performances of the work that I either saw or listened to seemed variations of that quintessentially classical production. When I saw the 1958 Salzburg production with Karl Böhm conducting and Elisabeth Schwarzkopf, Christa Ludwig, Rolando Panerai, Luigi Alva, and Graziella Sciutti in the cast, I took it to be an elaboration of the Metropolitan realization.

Even though I am neither a professional musicologist nor a Mozart scholar, it has seemed to me that most, if not all, interpretations of the opera stress the aspects picked up and magnified by Lunt: the work's effervescent, rollicking, courtly fun, the apparent triviality of its plot and its silly characters, and the astonishing beauty of its music, especially in the ensembles. Although I have always wanted to see any production of *Così fan tutte*, I have also resigned myself to performances that remained firmly grooved in *that* particular mode, which has never really convinced me that it was the right one for this superb yet elusive and somewhat mysterious opera. The only departure from the pattern was Peter Sellars's production of *Così fan tutte*, staged along with the two other Mozart–Da Ponte collaborations at the now defunct Pepsico Summerfare in Purchase, New York, in the late 1980s. The great virtue of those productions was that all the eighteenth-century clichés were simply swept away. Sellars argued that, just as Mozart wrote the operas while the ancien régime was crumbling, they should be set by contemporary directors at a similar moment in our own time, with the crumbling of the American empire alluded to by characters and settings, as well as by class deformations and personal histories that bore the marks of a society in crisis. Thus Sellars's version of *Le nozze di Figaro* (1786) takes place in the overblown luxury of the Trump Tower; *Don Giovanni* (1787) on a poorly lit street in Spanish Harlem, where dealers and junkies transact their business; and *Così fan tutte* in Despina's Diner, where a group of Vietnam veterans and their girlfriends hang out, play tricky games, and get frighteningly embroiled in feelings and self-discoveries that they are unprepared for and largely incapable of dealing with.

So far as I know, no one except Sellars has attempted such a full-scale revisionist interpretation of Mozart's three Da Ponte operas, which remain in the repertory as essentially courtly, classical eighteenth-century operas. Even Salzburg's 1994 Patrice Chéreau production of *Don Giovanni*—despite its striking savagery and relentlessly obsessive pace—functions within what we take to be Mozart's strictly conventional eighteenth-century theatrical idiom. What makes Sellars's productions of the three operas so powerful is that they put the viewer directly in touch with what is most eccentric and opaque about Mozart: the obsessive patterning in the operas, patterning that has little to do with showing that crime doesn't pay or that the faithlessness inherent in all human beings must be overcome before true union can occur.

Mozart's characters in *Don Giovanni* and *Così fan tutte* can indeed be interpreted not just as individuals with definable biographies and characteristics, but as figures driven by forces outside themselves that they don't comprehend and make no serious effort to understand. These operas, in fact, are much more about power and manipulation than they are given credit for by most opera directors or audiences. In them, individuality is reduced to a momentary identity in the impersonal rush of things. There is little room, therefore, for providence, or for the heroics of charismatic personalities, although Don Giovanni himself cuts a defiant and dashing figure within a very limited scope. Compared with the operas of Beethoven, Verdi, or even Rossini, Mozart depicts an amoral Lucretian world in which power has its own logic, undomesticated either by conditions of piety or verisimilitude. As much as he seems to have looked down on Mozart's lack of seriousness, Wagner shared a similar worldview, I think, and that is one of the reasons that his characters in the *Der Ring des Nibelungen*, *Tristan und Isolde*, and *Parsifal* spend as much as time as they do going over, renarrating, and recomprehending the remorseless chain of actions in which they are imprisoned and from which there can be no significant escape. What is it that keeps Don Giovanni irrecusably bound to his licentiousness—exposed with such cold, quantitative precision in Leporello's aria "Madamina, il catalogo è questo"—or *Così*'s Don Alfonso and Despina to their schemes and fixings? Little in the operas themselves provides an immediate answer.

Indeed, I think Mozart has tried to embody an abstract force that drives people by means of agents (in *Così fan tutte*) or sheer energy (in *Don Giovanni*), without the reflective consent of their mind or will in most instances. The intrigue in *Così fan tutte* is the result of a bet between Alfonso on the one hand and Ferrando and Guglielmo on the other, inspired neither by a sense of moral purpose nor by ideological passion. Ferrando is in love with Dorabella, Guglielmo with Fiordiligi; Alfonso bets that the women will be unfaithful. A subterfuge is then enacted: the two men will pretend that they have been called off to war.

Then they will come back in disguise and woo the girls, which is what happens. As Albanian (i.e., oriental) men, the two attempt to seduce each other's fiancée: Guglielmo quickly succeeds with Dorabella; Ferrando needs more time, but he too is successful with Fiordiligi, who is clearly the more serious of the two sisters. Alfonso is helped in the plot by Despina, a cynical maid who assists in her mistresses' downfall, although she does not know of the bet among the men. Finally the plot is exposed, the women are furious, but they return to their lovers, even though Mozart does not specify exactly whether the pairs remain as they were at the outset.

As many commentators have noted, the opera's plot has antecedents in various "test" plays and operas. As Charles Rosen accurately says, it resembles "demonstration" plays written by Marivaux among others. "They demonstrate—prove by acting out—psychological ideas and 'laws' that everyone accepted," Rosen adds, "and they are almost scientific in the way they show precisely how these laws work in practice."[1] He goes on to speak of *Così fan tutte* as "a closed system"—an interesting if insufficiently developed notion, which does in fact apply to the opera.[2]

We can learn a good deal more about *Così fan tutte* in the late eighteenth-century cultural setting by looking at Beethoven's reactions to the Da Ponte operas, which, as an Enlightenment enthusiast, Beethoven seems always to have regarded with a certain amount of discomfort. Like many critics of Mozart's operas, Beethoven is (so far as I have been able to discover) curiously silent about *Così fan tutte*. To generations of Mozart admirers, including Beethoven, the opera seems to refuse the kind of metaphysical, social, or cultural significance found readily by Kierkegaard and other luminaries in *Don Giovanni*, *Die Zauberflöte*, and *Figaro*. Therefore, there seems very little to say about it. Most people concede that the music is extremely wonderful, but the unsaid implication is that it is wasted on a silly story, silly characters, and an even sillier setting. Significantly enough, Beethoven seems to have thought *Die Zauberflöte* (1791) the greatest of Mozart's works—mainly because it was a German work—and he is quoted by his contemporaries Ignaz von Seyfried, Ludwig Rellstab, and Franz Wegeler as expressing his dislike of *Don Giovanni* and *Figaro*; they were too trivial, too Italian, too scandalous for a serious composer.[3] Once, however, he expressed pleasure at *Don Giovanni*'s success, although he was also said not to have wanted to attend Mozart's operas because they might make him forfeit his own originality.[4]

These are the contradictory feelings of a composer who found Mozart's work as a whole unsettling and even disconcerting. Competitiveness is clearly a factor, but there is something else. It is Mozart's uncertain moral center, the absence in *Così fan tutte* of a specific humanistic message of the kind about which *Die Zauberflöte* is so laboriously explicit. What is still more significant about Beethoven's reactions to Mozart is that *Fidelio* can be interpreted as a direct and, in my opinion, a somewhat desperate response to *Così fan tutte*. Take one small but certainly telling example: *Fidelio*'s heroine Leonore appears at the outset disguised as a young man, "Fidelio," who comes to work as an assistant at the prison where her husband, Florestan, is being held as a political prisoner by a tyrannical governor, Don Pizarro. In this guise, Leonore engages the amorous attentions of Marzelline, the daughter of the prison's guard, Rocco. You could say that Beethoven has picked up a bit of the *Così* plot, in which the disguised lovers return to Naples and proceed to make advances to the wrong women. However, no sooner does the intrigue start up than Beethoven puts a stop to it, revealing to the audience that young Fidelio is really the ever faithful and constant Leonore, who has come to Don Pizarro's prison to assert her fidelity and conjugal love to her imprisoned husband.

Nor is this all. Leonore's central aria, "Komm, Hoffnung," is full of echoes of Fiordiligi's "Per pietà, ben mio, perdona" in act 2 of *Così*. Fiordiligi sings this aria as a last, forlorn plea to herself to remain constant and to drive away the dishonor she feels might be overcoming her as she suffers (and perhaps slightly enjoys) the impress of Ferrando's importuning: "Svenerà quest'empia voglia / L'ardir mio, la mia costanza, / Perderà la rimembranza / Che vergogna e orror mi fa" (My courage, my constancy, will bleed dry this wicked desire and banish the memory which fills me with shame and horror). Memory is something to be banished, the memory she is ashamed of: her trifling with her real but absent lover Guglielmo. Yet memory is also what she must try to hold on to, the guarantee of her loyalty to her lover—for if she forgets, she loses the ability to judge her present, timidly flirtatious behavior for the shameful wavering it really is. Mozart gives her a noble, horn-accompanied figure for this avowal, a melody to be echoed in both key (E major) and instrumentation (horns) in Leonore's great appeal to hope: "Lass den letzten Stern / Der Müden nicht erbleichen" (Let this last star for the weary not be extinguished). But, although like Fiordiligi, Leonore has a secret, hers is an honorable one, and she does not doubt hope and love—she depends on them. There is no wavering, no doubting or timidity in Leonore, and her powerful aria, with its battery of horns proclaiming her determination and resolve, seems almost like a reproach to Fiordiligi's rather more delicate and troubled musings. Fiordiligi ends her aria on a note of regret, since she has already embarked on her course of betrayal, whereas Leonore is beginning her own ordeal of constancy and redemption on behalf of her still-missing husband.

Doubtless, in *Fidelio* Beethoven wrestled with various issues that were important to him independently of *Così*, but I think we have to grant that something about the world of Mozart's mature and greatest operas (with the exception of *Die Zauberflöte*) kept bothering Beethoven. One aspect is their sunny, comic, and southern setting, which amplifies and makes more difficult to accept their underlying critique and implied rejection of the middle-class virtue that seems to have meant so much to Beethoven. Even *Don Giovanni*, the one Da Ponte opera whose twentieth-century reinterpretations have turned it into a "northern" psychodrama of neurotic drives and transgressive passions, is essentially more unsettlingly powerful when enacted as a comedy of heedlessness and enjoyable insouciance. The style of famous twentieth-century Italian Dons like Ezio Pinza, Tito Gobbi, and Cesare Siepi prevailed until the 1970s, but their characterizations have given way to those of Thomas Allen, James Morris, Ferruccio Furlanetto, and Samuel Ramey, who represent the Don as a dark figure heavily influenced by readings in Kierkegaard and Freud. *Così fan tutte* is even more aggressively "southern" in that all its Neapolitan characters are depicted as being shifty, pleasure centered, and, with the exception of a brief moment here and there, selfish and relatively free of guilt, even though what they do is, by *Fidelio*'s standards, patently reprehensible.

Thus the earnest, heavy, and deeply serious atmosphere of *Fidelio* can be seen as a reproach to *Così*, which for all its irony and beauty—well described by critics like Charles Rosen and Scott Burnham—is grippingly without any kind of gravity at all.[5] When the two pseudo-oriental suitors are repulsed by Fiordiligi and Dorabella at the end of act 1, they drag the sisters into a broadly comic, false suicide scene. What transpires is based on the ironic disparity between the women's earnest concern for the men and the two suitors' amused playacting, with Despina's pretending to be a Mesmer-like "medico" whom the women can't understand ("parla un linguaggio che non sappiamo") added on for good measure. Genuine emotion is thus undercut by the ridiculousness of what is going on. In act 2, where the disguises and playacting advance quite significantly into the emotions of the four main characters, Mozart extends the joke even further. The result is that the four do fall in love again, though with the wrong partners, and this undermines something very dear to Beethoven: constancy of identity. Whereas Leonore takes on the mask of the boy Fidelio, her disguise is designed to get her closer to, not further away from, her real identity as faithful wife. Indeed, all the characters in *Fidelio* are rigorously circumscribed in their unvarying essence: Pizarro as unyielding villain, Florestan as champion of good, Fernando as emissary of light, and so forth. This is at the opposite pole from *Così*, where disguises and the wavering and wandering they foster are the norm, constancy and stability mocked at as impossible. Despina puts it quite explicitly in act 2: "Quello ch'è stato, è stato, / Scordiamci del passato. / Rompasi omai quel laccio, / Segno di servitù" (What's done is done, let's forget about the past. Let that bond be broken already, a symbol of servitude).

Still, *Così fan tutte* is an opera whose strange lightheartedness hides, or at least makes light of, an inner system that is quite severe and amoral in its workings. I do not at all want to say that the work must not be enjoyed as the brilliant romp that in many ways it surely is. The critic's role, however, is to try to lay bare what it is that Mozart and Da Ponte were intimating through their merry tale of deceit and displaced love. R. P. Blackmur quite rightly says that "the critic brings to consciousness the means of performance."[6] I shall therefore try to elucidate the way in which *Così fan tutte* is, at its concealed limits, a very different work than its rollicking exterior and sublime music suggests—although part of the joy is how, in bringing to consciousness the means of Mozart's and Da Ponte's performance, we appreciate and derive pleasure from the contradictory ways the opera unfolds before us in the theater.

Thanks to Alan Tyson's careful research, we now know that Mozart composed the ensembles of *Così* before he took on the arias and even the overture.[7] This sequence corresponds to the opera's concentration on relationships between characters rather than on brilliant individuals as encountered in earlier operas such as *Figaro* or *Don Giovanni*. Of the three Da Ponte operas, *Così fan tutte* is not only the last and, in my opinion, the most complex and eccentric, but also the most internally well organized, the most full of echoes and references, and the most difficult to unlock—precisely because it goes subtly further toward the limits of acceptable, ordinary experiences of love, life, and ideas than either of its two predecessors. The reasons for this, and indeed for *Così*'s opacity and even resistance to the kind of political and intellectual interpretive analysis that *Figaro* and *Don Giovanni* generally permit, are partly to be found in Mozart's life and times in 1789, while he was at work on *Così*. But they are also to be found in the way Mozart and Da Ponte created the work together, without a well-known play or a legendary figure to provide them with framework and directions. *Così* is the result of a collaboration, and its dynamics, the symmetrical structure of its plot, and the echoic quality of so much of its music are internal factors of its composition, not imported into or imposed on it by an outside source.

Many of the numbers of act 1, for example, are written by Mozart to emphasize how the characters think, act, and sing in pairs; their lines generally imitate one another and recollect lines sung earlier. Mozart seems to want us to feel we are inside a closed system in which melody, imitation, and parody are very difficult to separate from one another. This is superbly in evidence in the act 1 sextet "Alla bella Despinetta," which enacts a sort of mini-play in which Alfonso draws Despina, then the two disguised men, then the two women into his plot, all the while commenting on the action, as he also allows Despina to comment. The whole number (written in the opera's basic key of C major) is a dizzying maze of advance and expostulation, statement, echo, and inversion that rivals anything Mozart ever wrote for elegance, invention, and complexity. It simply sweeps aside the last trace of any sense of stability and gravity that we have so far been able to hold on to.

Yet to encounter *Così* today, either on disc or in the theater, is with few exceptions to risk not becoming aware of how carefully Mozart intended all of this. Opera is experienced in the theater as a basically undramatic, albeit theatrical and extravagant form. Most spectators do not understand the language, and if they do, they cannot understand the singers. In addition, *Così* has an aggressively silly, inconsequential plot that is enacted by characters who seem to have no interesting past to unravel or expose, and no encumbering relationships that claim their loyalty and the investment of their emotions. Surface seems to be all, except for the music, which is dazzling. Our contemporary social framework, and what Adorno called "the regression of listening," operates to sever music from drama and language.[8] We tend to think of opera as a series of arias or tunes connected to each other by a generally stupid, melodramatic, or unreal kind of story, in which we listen to the music in spite of the ridiculous and probably irrelevant goings-on on the stage. Some composers, Wagner most prominently, carry with them an aura of profundity or at least significance of the kind that he himself took great pains in his prose works to elaborate and to ascribe to his operas. But not even many Wagnerites carry his ideas in their mind when they see performances of *Lohengrin* or *Tristan* at the opera house; those performances are part of what is called "opera," a not quite rational, emotive form that is less serious than drama and of somewhat more consequence than musical comedy. What seems to me the one absolutely central and radical question about opera is: "Why do these people sing?" Yet in the conditions under which operas are performed today—as hugely expensive, lumbering projects that are curatorially rendered as pertaining to a distant, largely irrecoverable past and to an eccentric, privileged, and unserious present—the question can scarcely be posed, much less answered.

Così fan tutte presents special problems, even in a setting like today's in which mindless productions resolutely stand against our own contemporary world of ideas and politics, reflecting only the tastes and prejudices of a small coterie that has decided to keep opera frozen in a harmless little box that can offend neither audiences nor corporate sponsors. To come to terms with *Così* is first of all to be reminded that, when it premiered in Vienna on January 26, 1790, it was a contemporary opera, not a classic as it has become today. Mozart worked at it during the first part of 1789, at a time when he had just passed through a period of great difficulty. Andrew Steptoe discusses the circumstances of the composer's life at the time of *Così*'s composition with great insight and tact, although like all other commentators he is obliged to rely on speculation, since the actual information we seem to have is unusually sparse.[9] Steptoe first of all points out that, after he had completed *Don Giovanni* in 1787, "Mozart's personal health and financial security deteriorated." Not only did a German tour he undertook fail, but he also seems to have passed through a "loss in creative confidence," composing very few works and leaving an unusual number of fragments and unfinished pieces. In particular, he had difficulties with the string quartets he was writing for Kaiser Friedrich Wilhelm, which he did not complete for over a year.[10]

We do not really know why he took up work on *Così fan tutte*, although Steptoe volunteers (correctly I think) that the piece "was therefore located at a pivotal moment, and must have been seized upon by the composer both as an artistic challenge and a golden opportunity to recoup financially."[11] The score that Mozart finally did produce bears the marks, I believe, of other aspects of his life in 1789. One (referred to by Steptoe) is his wife Constanze's absence for a rest cure in Baden while he worked on the opera. While there, she "displayed improprieties" that prompted a letter from Mozart casting himself as the constant one, his wife as the flighty, embarrassing partner who needs to be *reminded*—the theme of remembering and forgetting is basic to *Così*—of her position and domestic status:

> Dear little wife! I want to talk to you quite frankly. You have no reason whatever to be unhappy! You have a husband who loves you and does all he possibly can for you. . . . I am glad indeed when you have some fun—of course I am—but I do wish that you would not sometimes make yourself so cheap. In my opinion you are far too free and easy with N.N. . . . . Now please remember that N.N. are not half so familiar with other women, whom they perhaps know more intimately, as they are with you. Why, N.N. who is usually a well-conducted fellow and particularly respectful to women, must have been misled by your behaviour into writing the most disgusting and most impertinent sottises which he put into his letter. A woman must always make herself respected, or else people will begin to talk about her. My love! Forgive me for being so frank, but my peace of mind demands it as

> well as our mutual happiness. Remember that you yourself once admitted to me that you were inclined to comply too easily. You know the consequences of that. Remember too the promises you gave to me. Oh, God, do try, my love![12]

How important Mozart's own almost Archimedean sense of stability and control was in dealing with Constanze is remarked by Steptoe, who argues that, because Mozart did not believe in "blind romantic love," he "satirised it mercilessly (most notably in *Così fan tutte*)."[13] Yet the letters from the *Così* period quoted by Steptoe tell a more complicated story. In one, Mozart tells Constanze how excited he is at the prospect of seeing her, and then adds: "If people could see into my heart, I should almost feel ashamed." We might then expect him to say something about seething passions and sensual thoughts. Instead he continues: "To me, everything is cold—cold as ice." And then he notes that "everything seems so empty." In a subsequent letter, Mozart speaks again of "feeling—a kind of emptiness, which hurts me dreadfully—a kind of longing, which is never satisfied, which never ceases, and which persists, nay rather increases daily."[14] In Mozart's correspondence there are other letters of this sort that characterize his special combination of unstilled energy—expressed in the sense of emptiness and unsatisfied longing that increases all the time—and cold control; these seem to me to have a particular relevance for the position of *Così fan tutte* in his life and oeuvre.

Figaro and *Don Giovanni* belong to the same group as *Così*, but whereas they are expansive, explicit, and intellectually and morally transparent, *Così* is concentrated, full of implicit and internalized characteristics, morally and politically limited, if not opaque. The third Da Ponte opera is also, relatively speaking, a late work, rather than just a mature one as its predecessors were. The opera's score is not only structured by the ensembles, but it looks back to earlier works and is full of "thematic reminiscences," as Steptoe calls them.[15] For instance, at one point in act I (Dorabella's accompanied recitative "Ah, scostati"), the orchestra suddenly plays the rapid scale passages associated with the Commendatore in *Don Giovanni*. Mozart's use of counterpoint gives the music added substance, so that in the A-flat canon in the second act's finale one experiences not only a remarkable sense of rigor, but also a special ironic expressiveness well beyond the words and the situation. For as the lovers have finally worked their way around to the new reversed pairing, three of them sing polyphonically of submerging all thought and memory in the wine they are about to drink, while only one, Guglielmo, remains disaffected—he had greater faith in Fiordiligi's power to resist Ferrando, but he has been disproved—and he stands outside the canon. He wishes that the women ("queste volpi senza onor"; these vixens without honor) would drink poison and end the whole thing. It is as if Mozart wanted the counterpoint to mirror the lovers' embarrassment in a closed polyphonic system, and also to show how even though they think of themselves as shedding all ties and memories, the music, by its circularity and echoic form, reveals them to be bound to each other in a new and logically consequent embrace.

Such a moment is unique to *Così fan tutte*: it depicts human desire and satisfaction in musical terms as essentially a matter of compositional control that directs feeling and appetite into a logical circuit allowing no escape and very little elevation. Guglielmo's bad-tempered, sour-grapes line further negates the consummation implied in the words. But the whole opera—plot, characters, situation, ensembles, and arias—tends to such a cluster as provided in this scene because it is derived from the movement of two intimate couples, two men and two women, plus two "outside" characters, coming together in various ways, and then pulling apart, then coming together again, with several changes along the way. The symmetries and repetitions are almost cloying, but they are the substance of the opera. We know very little about these figures; no traces of a former life adhere to them (unlike the characters in *Figaro* and *Don Giovanni*, who are steeped in earlier episodes, entanglements, intrigues); their identities exist in order to be tested and exercised as lovers, and once they have gone through one full turn so that they become the opposite of what they were, the opera ends. The overture, with its busy, clattering, round-like themes, catches this spirit quite perfectly. Remember that Mozart wrote it after he had finished most of the main body of the opera—that is, after the schematic character of what he was elaborating had impressed itself on his mind.

Only one figure, Don Alfonso, stands apart from all this. His is the only activity that begins before the opera opens. In *Così*'s opening trio, which seems to be the continuation of an argument already begun, Ferrando and Guglielmo refer to Alfonso's antecedent comment that "detto ci avete che infide esser ponno" (you've told us they could be untrustworthy)—and it continues uninterruptedly to the very end. Who is he really?

He certainly belongs to a line of senior authority figures who dot Mozart's life and works. Remember the Commendatore in *Don Giovanni*, or Sarastro in *Die Zauberflöte*, or even Bartolo and Almaviva in *Figaro*. Yet Alfonso's role is different from the others in that he seeks to prove, not the underlying moral fiber, but the inconstancy and unfaithfulness of women—and he succeeds, initiating the four lovers into a life of reason and undeceived love. In the final ensemble, when he is denounced by the women as the man who misled them and managed their fall, Alfonso responds without a trace of regret. What he has done, he says, is to have *undeceived* them, and this, he adds, puts them more under his command: "V'ingannai, ma fu l'inganno / Disinganno ai vostri amanti, / Che più saggi omai saranno, / Che faran quel ch'io vorrò" (I deceived you, but my deception was disillusionment for your lovers, who from now on will be wiser, and will do what I want). "Embrace each other and be silent," he then says, so that "all four of you now laugh, as I have laughed already and will laugh again." It is interesting and not entirely a coincidence that what he sings contains striking anticipations of *Die Zauberflöte*, an opera that Mozart seems to have written as a more morally acceptable version of the same demonstration or test story used in *Così fan tutte*. Whereas in *Così* constancy does not win out, in *Die Zauberflöte* it does.

Like Sarastro in *Die Zauberflöte*, Don Alfonso is a manager and controller of behavior, although unlike Sarastro he acts with neither solemnity nor high moral purpose. Most accounts of *Così* scarcely pay attention to him, and yet in the unguardedly amoral world of the opera he is not only a crucial and indeed the pivotal figure but a fascinating one as well. His many references to himself—actor, teacher, scholar (the various Latin tags and classical references suggest a good education), plotter, courtier—do not directly allude to the one thing he seems above all to be: a mature libertine, someone who has had lots of worldly sexual experience and now wishes to direct, control, and manipulate the experience of others. In this he resembles an amiable schoolmaster, a military strategist, and a philosopher; he has seen much in the world and is more than able to stage another drama of the sort he has presumably lived through himself. He knows in advance what conclusion he will come to, so the action of the opera furnishes him with few surprises, least of all about how women behave. In the agitated little passage in act 1 "Nel mare solca," he speaks of plowing the sea, sowing on sand, trying to ensnare the wind in a net: these impossibilities define the limits of Alfonso's reality, and they accentuate the element of radical instability in which, as a teacher of lovers and a practiced lover himself, he lives. But this apparently does not prevent him from enjoying both the experience of loving and the experience of proving his ideas that he sets up in order to demystify love for his four young friends.

I do not want to suggest that Don Alfonso is anything other than comic figure. But I do want to argue that he stands very close to a number of cultural and psychological actualities that meant a great deal to Mozart, as well as to other relatively advanced thinkers and artists of the time. Consider first the unmistakable progression in Mozart's operatic invention from Figaro to Don Giovanni to Don Alfonso. Each in his own way is unconventional and iconoclastic, although only Don Alfonso is neither punished, like Don Giovanni, nor in effect domesticated, as Figaro is. The discovery that the stabilities of marriage and the social norms habitually governing human life are inapplicable, because life itself is as elusive and inconstant as his experience teaches, makes of Don Alfonso a character in a new, more turbulent and troubling realm, one in which experience repeats the same disillusioning patterns without relief. What he devises for the two pairs of lovers is a game in which human identity is shown to be as protean, unstable, and undifferentiated as anything in the actual world.

Not surprisingly, then, one of the main motifs in *Così fan tutte* is the elimination of memory so that only the present is left standing. The structure of the plot, with its play-within-a-play abstractions, enforces that: Alfonso sets up a test, which separates the lovers from their past and their loyalties. Then the men assume new identities and return to woo and finally win the women. Despina is also brought in, although she and Alfonso remain emotionally detached from the two central pairs. But the net effect of this is that Ferrando and Guglielmo enter into their new roles as much as the women, take seriously their charge as lovers, and in the process prove what Alfonso knew all along. Yet Guglielmo is not so easily resigned to Fiordiligi's apparent fickleness and therefore remains for a time outside Alfonso's circle of happy, and deceived, lovers. Despite his bitterness, however, Guglielmo rallies round to Alfonso's thesis, given full articulation in the opera for the first time toward the end of act 2, in "Tutti accusan le donne." This statement by Alfonso is in C major, the basic key of the opera; its climax is built on a rudimentary harmonic progression; and its style is both academic and—for Mozart—extremely plain. This is a late moment in the opera. Alfonso has been biding his time before putting things as flatly, in as unadorned and reductive a manner as this. It is as if he, and Mozart, needed act 1 to set up the demonstration, and act 2 to let it spin itself out, before he could come forward with this conclusion, which is also the musical root, finally revealed, of the opera.

Alfonso represents the standpoint not just of a jaded, illusionless man of the world, but also of an indefatigable practitioner and rigorous, albeit only partially involved, teacher of his views—a figure who apparently needs subjects and space for his demonstrations, even though he knows in advance that the pleasures he sets up are far from new. They may be exciting and amusing, but they simply confirm that about which he has no doubt. In this respect Don Alfonso resembles an understated version of his near contemporary the Marquis de Sade, a libertine who, as Foucault describes him memorably,

> is he who, while yielding to all the fantasies of desire and to each of its furies, can, but also must, illumine their slightest movement with a lucid and deliberately elucidated representation. There is a strict order governing the life of the libertine: every representation must be immediately endowed with life in the living body of desire, every desire must be expressed in the pure light of representative discourse [in this case, in act 2, the language or discourse of love]. Hence the rigid sequence of "scenes" (the scene, in Sade, is profligacy subjected to the order of representation) and, within the scenes, the meticulous balance between the conjugation of bodies and the concentration of reasons.[16]

We recall that in the opera's first number, Alfonso speaks "ex cathedra," as a man with gray hair and long experience; we are to assume, I think, that having yielded to desire in the past, he is now ready to illuminate his ideas with what Foucault calls "a lucid and deliberately elucidated representation," which of course is the comedy he imposes on Guglielmo and Ferrando.[17] The plot of *Così* is a rigid sequence of scenes, all of them manipulated by Alfonso and Despina, his equally cynical helper, in which sexual desire is, as Foucault suggests, profligacy subjected to the order of representation—that is, the enacted tale of lovers being schooled in an illusionless yet exciting love. When the game is revealed to Fiordiligi and Dorabella, they accept the truth of what they have experienced and, in a conclusion that has troubled interpreters and directors with its coy ambiguity, they sing of reason and mirth without any specific indication at all from Mozart that the two women and two men will return to their original lovers.

Such a conclusion opens up a troubling vista of numerous further substitutions, with no ties, no identity, no idea of stability or constancy left undisturbed. Foucault speaks of this cultural moment as one in which language retains the capacity to name, but can only do so in a "ceremony reduced to the utmost precision . . . and extends it to infinity." The lovers will go on finding other partners, since the rhetoric of love and the representation of desire have lost their anchors in a fundamentally unchanging order of Being: "Our thought is so brief, our freedom so enslaved, our discourse so repetitive, that we must face the fact that that expanse of shade below is really a bottomless sea."[18] It is against this rather dreadful vista that Mozart permits only one character, Guglielmo, to rage openly in his harsh and yet aggressively charming patter aria "Donne mie, la fate a tanti" in act 2.

Don Alfonso is responsible for that rage, a parodic Virgil leading young, inexperienced men and women into a world stripped of standards, norms, and certainties. He speaks the language of wisdom and sagacity, allied to an admittedly small-scaled and limited vision of his power and control. There are plenty of classical references in the libretto, but none of them refers to the Christian or Masonic deities that Mozart seems to have venerated elsewhere. (He became a Mason in 1784.) Don Alfonso's natural world is in part Rousseau's, stripped of sanctimonious piety, volatile with fancy and caprice, made rigorous with the need to experience desire without palliatives or conclusion. Even more significantly for Mozart, Don Alfonso is only the second authority figure in his operas to appear after the death of Mozart's father, Leopold, in 1787. Given some urgency by his death, the terrifying Commendatore in *Don Giovanni* embodies the stern, judgmental aspect of Leopold's relationship with his son (discussed by Maynard Solomon so illuminatingly as an obsessively desired master/bondsman relationship in Mozart's thought)—something not at all present in Alfonso, who is not easily provoked, gives every appearance of wanting to play the game with his young friends, and seems completely untroubled by the pervasive faithlessness that his "scenes" have uncovered.[19]

Alfonso, I believe, is an irreverent and later portrait of the senior patron, someone quite audaciously presented not as a moral instructor but as an amorous virtuoso, a libertine or a retired rake whose influence is exerted through hoaxes, disguises, charades, and finally a philosophy of inconstancy as norm. Because he is an older and more resigned man, Alfonso intimates a sense of mortality that is very far from the concerns of the young lovers. A famous letter written by Mozart to his father in the final period of the latter's life, on April 4, 1787, expresses this mood of illusionless fatalism:

> As death, when we come to consider it closely, is the true goal of our existence, I have formed during the last few years such close relations with this best and truest friend of mankind, that his image is not only no longer terrifying to me, but is indeed very soothing and consoling! . . . Death is the *key* which unlocks the door to our true happiness. I never lie down at night without reflecting that—young as I am—I may not live to see another day.[20]

Death is rendered here less formidable and intimidating than it is for most people. This is not a conventionally Christian sentiment, however, but a naturalist one: death as something familiar and even dear, as a door to other experiences. Yet death is also represented as an inducement to a sense of fatalism and lateness—that is, the feeling that one is late in life, and the end is near.

So also in *Così fan tutte* the father figure has become the friend and cheerful, tyrannical mentor, a person to be obeyed who is somehow neither paternalistic nor minatory. And this status is confirmed in Mozart's style, in which posturing characters are displayed and presented in such a way as to permit

Alfonso's ideas to enter into a game with them, not as a hectoring senior presence nor as an admonishing pedagogue, but as an actor in the common entertainment. Alfonso predicts the conclusion or end of the comedy. But here, according to Donald Mitchell,

> we stumble, I believe, on the most uncomfortable aspect of the opera's factuality. What we yearn for is the possibility of a fairy-tale reconciliation. But Mozart was far too truthful an artist to disguise the fact that a healing forgiveness is impossible where all the parties [Alfonso included] are not only equally "guilty" but share to the full the knowledge of each other's guilt. In *Così*, the best that can be done is to present as brave a front as one may to the facts of life [and, I could add, of death]. The coda that succeeds the *dénouement* does exactly that and no more.[21]

The conclusion of *Così* is really twofold: this is the way things are because that is what *they* do, *così fan tutte*, and, second, they *will be* like that, one situation, one substitution, succeeding another, until by implication the process is stopped by death. All are the same, *così fan tutte*, in the meantime. In the aria "Come scoglio" in act 1, Fiordiligi says: "E potrà la morte sola / Far che cangi affetto il cor" (Death alone will be able to make the heart change its affection). Death takes the place of Christian reconciliation and redemption, the key to our true—if unknown and indescribable—hope of rest and stability, soothing and consoling without providing anything more than a theoretical intimation of final repose.

But, like nearly every serious subject with which the opera flirts, death is kept at bay—indeed, is mostly left out of *Così fan tutte*. Here we should recall those extraordinary feelings of solitary longing and coldness about which Mozart spoke while he worked on the opera. What affects us about *Così* is, of course, the wonderful music, which often seems so incongruously more interesting than the situation Mozart uses it for, except when (especially in act 2) the four lovers express their complex feelings of elation, regret, fear, and outrage. But even at such moments, the disparity between Fiordiligi's assertion of faith and devotion in "Come scoglio" and the genuinely frivolous game she is involved in deflates the noble sentiments and music she utters. This disparity makes her music seem both impossibly overstated and sensationally beautiful at the same time—a combination, I think, that corresponds to Mozart's feelings of unsatisfied longing and cold mastery. Listening to her aria and seeing the hubbub of serious and comic elements jostling each other on the stage, we are kept from wandering off into either speculation or despair, obligated to follow the tight discipline of Mozart's rigor.

Within its carefully circumscribed limits, *Così fan tutte* allows itself only a number of gestures toward what stands just beyond it—or, to vary the metaphor a bit, through what stands just inside it. Mozart never ventured so close to the potentially terrifying view he and Da Ponte seem to have uncovered of a universe shorn of any redemptive or palliative scheme, whose one law is motion and instability expressed as the power of libertinage and manipulation, and whose only conclusion is the terminal repose provided by death. That so astonishingly satisfying a musical score should be joined to so heedless and insignificant a tale is what *Così fan tutte* accomplishes with such unique virtuosity. But I think we should not believe that the candid fun of the work does any more than hold its ominous vision in abeyance—that is, for as long as *Così fan tutte*'s limits are not permitted to invade the stage.

Chapter Two

FIDELIO'S DIFFICULTIES WITH THE PAST

EVEN WHEN it is performed indifferently, *Fidelio* is the one opera in the repertory that has the power to sway audiences by virtue of its passion, its tremendous moral and political affirmations about freedom and fidelity, and, of course, its superbly powerful and heroic music. Nevertheless, a close analysis reveals that *Fidelio* is, in fact, a highly problematic though deeply interesting work whose triumphant conclusion and the impression it is designed to convey of goodness winning out over evil do not go to the heart of what I believe Beethoven was grappling with. Not that its plot is complex, or that, like many of the French operas of the day that influenced Beethoven and whose brilliance he admired, it is long and complicated; *Fidelio*'s success in the theater derives in part from its compactness and its white-hot intensity, in which during the course of two extremely taut acts a devoted wife rescues her unjustly imprisoned husband, foils a tyrannically cruel Spanish grandee, and manages also to release all the other arbitrarily punished prisoners in his dungeons. Unlike most other operas, however, *Fidelio* is burdened with the complexities of its own past as well as the huge effort it cost its composer before he was able to present it in Vienna in its "final" form on May 23, 1814. It is the only work of its kind he ever completed, the one on which he lavished a great deal of pain and attention, and that he cared about very genuinely without perhaps getting the satisfaction from it, either by popular success or aesthetic conviction, that his efforts entitled him to.

What we know today as *Fidelio* is the third version of a three-act opera originally produced as *Leonore* in 1805, then again in a somewhat truncated two-act version in 1806, and finally in an even more edited and reconfigured two-act version as *Fidelio* in 1814. Nor is this all. *Fidelio* must be the only opera whose composer wrote for it no less than four overtures (three to *Leonore* and one to *Fidelio*); these works are still played in the concert hall, although, ironically, of the four only the overture to *Fidelio* makes no musical reference to the opera itself. Through the efforts of musicologists and musicians there now exists a fairly accurate composite version of the 1805–1806 *Leonore,* which in recent years has been both performed and recorded. Indeed, I know of two important occasions in 1996, once in New York and then some weeks later in Salzburg, when *Leonore* was performed in a lean, semi-staged concert rendition by conductor John Eliot Gardiner and his period-instrument Orchestre Révolutionnaire et Romantique. These performances were followed in Salzburg by Georg Solti conducting several staged performances of *Fidelio*, and in New York by Kurt Masur and the New York Philharmonic doing one extremely loud and stodgy concert version of it, which, in my opinion, highlighted Gardiner's much more dynamic conception and execution.

The force of Gardiner's commitment to *Leonore* as a more interesting work than *Fidelio* was buttressed by a spirited essay that he wrote for the New York program booklet. "With the *Leonore* of 1805," Gardiner suggests, "Beethoven was struggling to recover the fiery revolutionary fervor and idealism of his Bonn years after the relatively cozy time he had been having in Vienna. If *Leonore* could be said to spring from that self which continually searches for the ideal in the face of fear, *Fidelio*, by contrast, represents Beethoven's more settled, static response to tyranny and injustice, freedom and self-sacrifice." *Leonore*'s effectiveness comes from the "power and purity of its emotion." A few sentences later, Gardiner is very harsh about *Fidelio*, which he claims reinforces "its abstract, collective and philosophical message" at the expense of "personal and human complexity." It was *Fidelio* and not *Leonore* that was, he says, "hijacked to honor Hitler's birthday" because of its "unfortunate nationalistic baggage," and *Fidelio* again that, along with Beethoven's *Germania* (1814) and *Wellington's Victory* (1813), put the remains of his heroic style at the service of reactionary trends in Europe. But Gardiner is certainly right to suggest that the 1814 *Fidelio*, its associations with the Congress of Vienna (1814–1815) lending weight to its authoritative density and tightly controlled mass, never satisfied Beethoven, who frequently thereafter complained that the work needed rewriting from the beginning, despite the inordinate labor he had already expended on it over a period of ten or eleven years. Thus Gardiner in conclusion: "It is a fallacy to claim that in *Fidelio* Beethoven in every case refined and strengthened his first idea." And this leads him to add "that there exists on Beethoven's part no final version that subsumes all that is good in the others."[1]

Whether or not we agree with Gardiner in his judgment in favor of *Leonore* over *Fidelio*, it is important to consider the later version as continuing developments that occur in the first, as a later opera therefore rather self-consciously encumbered with its own past, one that persists as a central theme in all three versions of the work—the sense, that is, that the past, whether the work's own past or that of Beethoven and his characters and music, is not something left behind or edited out, but is both untidy and uncomfortable, that keeps encroaching upon the present, that will not settle down and cooperate, that keeps coming back to unsettle and dislocate the certainties and finalities of the "rescue opera" form that Beethoven was using. My reading of *Fidelio* sees the later version as extending and deepening rather than ending the struggle or work in progress that Gardiner discerns in *Leonore*.

Maynard Solomon notes that 1813 was an unproductive year for Beethoven, immediately after which he resorted to an "ideological/heroic" manner that yielded a series of noisily inferior works "filled with bombastic rhetoric and 'patriotic' excesses" that "mark the nadir of Beethoven's artistic career."[2] Such works as *Wellington's Victory* and several compositions written for the Congress of Vienna belong to the same period as the revisions to *Leonore* that resulted in the 1814 *Fidelio*. Solomon suggests that this ideological heroic style can be traced back to the 1790s, in the *Joseph* and *Leopold* cantatas (1790) as well as the

Friedelberg war songs (1796–1797); yet in central works—Solomon in particular cites the Third and Fifth Symphonies (1804 and 1808), *Fidelio*, and the incidental music to Goethe's *Egmont* (1810)—this aggressive and quasi-militaristic style "was sublimated into a subtle and profound form of expression."[3] It is, therefore, not surprising that *Fidelio*, as the last work in this series, explicitly recalls some of its predecessors, perhaps as part of its obsession with the past. A well-known example occurs in the final scene of act 2. Given permission by Don Fernando to release her husband Florestan from his chains, Leonore steps forward to perform the task of liberation. The music modulates from A major to F major and proceeds to a moving oboe solo and chorus borrowed almost literally from the *Cantata on the Death of Emperor Joseph II* (1790); in the opera, the episode bestows a majestic sense of order and calm on what has so far been a turbulent and confused scene. And—a second example—in the final moments of the opera it is hard not to hear echoes of the finale of the Fifth Symphony, animated and enlivened by words and voices. In both cases there is a similar, poundingly insistent use of C major to make affirmations and possess the tonic so as to dispel any lingering shadows.

Fidelio can also be interpreted as a terrific counterblow to Mozart's *Così fan tutte,* whose traces as an important antecedent are part of the past that Beethoven is working with. On the one hand, Beethoven incorporates the disguises, if not the malice, of *Così*; on the other, he uses unmasking as a way of asserting the virtues of the bourgeois matrimonial ideal of constancy in adversity. Memory in *Così fan tutte* is a faculty to be done away with in the pursuit of pleasure, whereas in *Fidelio* it is a vital part of character and constancy. Yet at the heart of the very thing that Beethoven is arguing for—persistence, the durability of fidelity, personal character as a source of continuity—there seems always to be a contradiction that will not disappear. It is lodged there as part of the very condition of its existence. Every affirmation, every instance of truth carries with it its own negation, just as every memory of love and conjugal fidelity also brings with it the danger and usually the actuality of something that will cancel it, annul it, obliterate it. Most critics who have written about Beethoven's powerfully heroic and teleological middle-period style—most recently Scott Burnham, but also Paul Robinson, for whom *Fidelio* is a relatively uncomplicated enactment of the French Revolution—seem to be more successful than Beethoven was in dispelling everything but the triumphalism with which he appears always to end his middle-period works.[4] If we look a bit more closely at *Fidelio*, however, with its background of incorporated and canceled earlier versions in mind, we will see a more gripping, much more ambiguous and self-conscious struggle going on, a struggle that I believe makes *Fidelio* a more challenging opera than it usually appears to be.

This struggle is evident from the beginning, when Jaquino and Marzelline spar over their future together (which Marzelline dreads because she has already fallen in love with her father's assistant, Fidelio—i.e., the disguised Leonore), although most commentators tend to treat the opening scene as being on an inferior level of seriousness and importance. But the scene, like most things in opera, is a hybrid, made up of elements that do not, because they cannot, blend; this produces a kind of volatility and tension that Beethoven throughout the opera is trying to represent. It derives at the outset from the incompatibility of desires and hopes: Jaquino's wanting at last to be alone with Marzelline, her pushing him away, Fidelio's interrupting their spat with insistent knocking. Each character has a different conception of time that does not mesh with those of the others: time is urgency for the eager young swain, hope for Marzelline, and, in Fidelio's case, anticipating and waiting. What is most symbolically freighted in the scene is Fidelio's first appearance, described meticulously by Beethoven: dressed as a young man, Fidelio carries a box of provisions on her back, a letter box on one arm, and, on her other arm, a collection of chains. We see the character, who is furnishing supplies and nourishment in the present, but also her encumbrances, which represent to her—as well as to her husband and perhaps the other prisoners—punishments brought on by past behavior.

The first appearance of Rocco, the prison guard, gives Beethoven an opportunity to tie together the four characters of the opening sequence using a canon at the octave, also instigated by the second-act canon of *Così fan tutte*. The idea of the canon is similar in both works, a sort of *discordia concors* in which the characters express their incompatible sentiments in a rigorous, albeit meditative and even scholastic form. Beethoven's canon "Mir ist so wunderbar" is significant for another reason, which takes us to the problematic of representation in *Fidelio* and the kind of irreconcilability I mentioned earlier as hampering, and certainly rendering difficult, the affirmations he seems to be trying to make in this last version of his only opera. His choice of Jean-Nicolas Bouilly's *Léonore, ou L'amour conjugal*, which Pierre Gaveaux had already set to music in 1798, provided him with an entirely predictable rescue plot, in which wrongs are righted and the prisoners made free. One of the things we respond to in *Fidelio*, more in the last version than in the earlier versions, is the force and the authority with which one form of power is dislodged and a new, or at least much more acceptable, one is established in its place. Pizarro, the tempestuously bloody-minded tyrant, is replaced by Don Fernando, emissary of light and truth. No reason or logic is given for this salutary change except that it emanates from an offstage source of goodness and justice, concealed from and inaccessible to Florestan, Leonore, Pizarro, and the rest. Fernando makes clear to us that he has been dispatched by the monarch and is therefore a deputy, or substitute.

It is far too easy and, I think, inaccurate to describe this rather slenderized politics as Beethoven's attempt to embody dramatically the enormous liberation he had once discerned in the French Revolution. There is something far too swift and almost magical about the opera to be, or represent, a political process. Unlike Wagner or even Mozart, Beethoven was neither particularly well read nor philosophically inclined. He read the great contemporary poets like Schiller and Goethe, but, when it came to philosophical ideas, attitudes about history, notions of universality, and human destiny, he was a relative freshman. The striving and pathos of *Fidelio* have more to do with the actual business of putting words and music together in the only work of its kind that he ever produced than with a historical event like the French Revolution or a general idea about humanity. The ready-made story offered by Bouilly and

Gaveaux was therefore a starting point for efforts to translate the wholly musical exertions he normally expended on his art into visual, verbal, and plastic terms, and this he found strange and difficult to do, especially when great emotions about a woman were involved. As all his biographers affirm, Beethoven was routinely moved by passions for unattainable women, especially during the period when he began to work on *Leonore*. As an instance of what this did to him, there is this fragment of a letter from 1805 to Countess Josephine Deym, a woman for whom he evinced the strongest emotion but who did not reciprocate the composer's advances:

> Why is there no language which can express what far above all mere regard—far above everything—that we can ever describe—Oh, who can name *you*—and not feel that however much he could speak about *you*—that would never attain—to *you*—only in music—Alas, am I not too proud when I believe that music is more at my command than words—*You*, *you*, my all, my happiness—alas, no—even in *my music* I cannot do so, although in this respect thou, Nature, has not stinted me with thy gifts. Yet there is too little for *you*.[5]

Without wishing to read too much of this turbulently inarticulate letter into the ungainly libretto for *Fidelio*, which was prepared by Joseph Sonnleithner, I still think that we can see in it something of the same travail experienced by Beethoven as he tried to transfer his musical impulses into the words and actions of the opera, the sense of a disparity between his musical competence and the consternation and overexcitement he felt as he articulated his feelings in melodic language. The purest example of this occurs in the powerful, yet strangely tongue-tied duet in act 2 between Florestan and Leonore, "O namenlose Freude." For the entire opera until this point, Florestan has been a hidden prisoner and Leonore has been disguised as a young man, involved both as Rocco's helper and as the illicit object of Marzelline's affection. Neither of the pair has been able to speak openly and clearly to the other. Then in the tempestuous dungeon quartet "Er sterbe" Leonore reveals herself, a magical trumpet call is heard twice, and it becomes clear to Pizarro that he and his evil plans have been defeated. Finally, the husband and wife face each other and in their duet they pour out their joyful love for each other. In *Leonore,* Beethoven had inserted a longish spoken interchange between husband and wife, each discovering the other, assuring themselves of their presence to each other, making the transition from a state of solitude and imprisonment to one of blissful union. In *Fidelio,* this is almost completely eliminated, and, although the sung duet in both versions is similar, the later music is more agitated and astringent.

There is no doubt that what Beethoven does in the earlier version of the opera at this point is humanly more acceptable and psychologically truer. But in keeping with so much of the later version, the dialogue by which the married couple is at last able to speak openly and without subterfuge is eliminated as a way of intensifying the present at the expense not only of a hindering past, but also of dramatic verisimilitude. It is as if Beethoven snatches the characters up from the dreary prison—so laboriously described and explored earlier in act 2—into another, higher, and even metaphysical realm where language and ordinarily declarative communication seem almost impossible. One of the most striking characteristics of the duet is the amount of hyperbole and exaggeration in it—joy is nameless, sorrows are untellable (*unnennbar*), happiness is overwhelming (*übergroß*). These expressions are repeated several times, giving the music of the duet that breathlessly stammering, but insistently excited and elevated quality that we find in the letter to Countess Deym. In addition, almost uniquely in the opera, the duet involves a relentlessly ascending, aspiring, striving motif, which is in striking contrast with the generally sighing, falling, and plaintive quality of the preceding music. Take as a contrasting instance the dungeon trio in act 2, in which Rocco and Fidelio, who are there to dig Florestan's grave, take pity on the forlorn and starved man and offer him food and drink. Beginning with Florestan's "Euch werde Lohn in bessern Welten" (May you be rewarded in better worlds), the trio is melodically shaped by the descending figures, usually seconds and thirds, that give the music its attractive pathos.

Then, too, there is the main theme of Florestan's aria at the beginning of act 2, where, while recollecting his early life in the desolate tranquility of Pizarro's dungeon, he also utilizes that basic descending figure, which is triply familiar because Beethoven used it as a motif in all three of the *Leonore* overtures. This passage is particularly worth looking at because, for the first time in the opera, Beethoven affords us only the most unsatisfactory glimmering of what Florestan's crime was. In act 1, Rocco, his altogether too accommodating and servile jailer, informs us only that the man is in prison because Florestan has powerful enemies. Now the prisoner himself avers that in his youth, "Wahrheit wagt ich kühn zu sagen, / Und die Ketten sind mein Lohn" (I bravely dared to speak the truth, and the chains are my reward). Beethoven gives us no indication at all what that truth is—except that it contained a denunciation of Pizarro's "treason" (which is unspecified)—though it is clear that what is Florestan's living grave, his death-in-life, has distanced him permanently from some irrecoverable, unrepeatable utterance in the past. Having once spoken that truth, Florestan cannot do so again, so rare and (to his worldly enemies) so threatening is it. We must assume that what Florestan said is political to some degree, as well as eloquent and dangerously effective; in the final scene, Don Fernando describes Florestan as a noble soul "der für Wahrheit stritt," who fought for truth. What exactly that truth is, however, is not disclosed, either in *Fidelio* or in its earlier versions. In all three versions of the work Florestan consoles himself for having done his duty ("meine Pflicht hab ich getan") in uttering that elusive truth, which nevertheless remains very much a political liability, an indescribable but deeply felt encumbrance in the past as well as present.

We must introduce a further complexity in this account of how Beethoven's various attempts at representing crucial feelings and statements in words and action falter so strikingly, and how he relies on the music to convey a sentiment or statement that is constitutively absent from the dramatic present. Only one character in the opera, Pizarro, fully inhabits and, of course, dominates the actions most of the time until his fall in act 2. It is *his* jail, *his* castle, *his* will; *his* servitors and prisoners are under *his* control, and, though he is a vengeful, cruel, and one-dimensional figure, he is clearly someone to be taken seriously. In his well-known study of *Fidelio,* Carl Dahlhaus notes that, whereas the lesser characters of the opera—Rocco, Marzelline, and Jaquino—try to create an idyll suited to their class-based tastes and predilections, Florestan and Leonore, who seem to belong to a higher class, strive on behalf of a utopia based on brotherhood and freedom.[6] Pizarro is the foil to both schemes. He breaks up the idyll by forcing the venial and temporizing Rocco into service as an accomplice to murder; and, so far as a political utopia is concerned, he is the embodiment of everything dystopic. There is a kind of almost sensual feeling he has for the present moment, which he regards as his self-fulfillment: he will be able to have his revenge on Florestan and at the same time revel in the pleasures of the act of killing itself.

Like so much else in the opera that is emphatically, indeed feverishly gestured at, none of this will come to pass. At the climactic moment of act 2, as Leonore and Rocco ready the grave and Pizarro prepares himself for his long-awaited moment of self-realization, Beethoven rather ingenuously engineers not only Leonore's brave interposition between her husband and Pizarro's bullet, but also the magically timed trumpet call during the great "Er Sterbe" quartet. More has been written about this episode in *Fidelio* than any other passage, for not only has the providential trumpet call been interpreted as a symbol of freedom, but also of hope, the new bourgeois world, the end of humanism, and so on. Characteristically, Adorno has one of the shrewder insights in his 1955 Darmstadt lecture on "Bourgeois Opera." I will not try to summarize the whole of his argument, except to say that his main point is to identify opera as a specifically bourgeois form. Here is the relevant passage on *Fidelio*'s trumpet call: "The fanfare of *Fidelio* also consummates almost ritualistically the moment of protest that breaks open the eternal hell of the prison cell and puts an end to the rule of force. This interlocking of myth and enlightenment defines the bourgeois essence of opera: namely, the interlocking of imprisonment in a blind and unselfconscious system and the idea of freedom, which arises in its midst."[7] This seems to me to grasp very accurately the singular abruptness that characterizes *Fidelio*'s style, very different in this respect from the more flowing, more humanly acceptable procedures of the opera's two earlier versions. John Eliot Gardiner's characterization of *Leonore* as a work in progress catches the sense of labor, development, and process that makes the earlier version so compelling to listen to; above all, in *Leonore* Beethoven seems much more interested in developing a set of relationships between the characters rather than a set of positions that they hold and declaim about. This is very evident in the quasi-domestic scenes of act I, in which Beethoven allows for a little foreplay—totally excised from *Fidelio*—between the lovestruck Marzelline and her father's ever so coy and evasive young assistant. The result of the abruptness in *Fidelio* is not simply the unmediated amalgam of enlightenment and magic that Adorno speaks about, but a strange, almost two-tiered style. On the one hand, Beethoven uses various numbers to advance the action: for example, the trio sung by Fidelio, Rocco, and Marzelline ("Gut, Söhnchen, gut") in act I that prepares Fidelio and Rocco to go down into the forbidden areas of the prison; and—a sort of continuation of the trio—the Rocco-Pizarro duet a few moments later, in which "der Gouverneur," as Rocco calls him, presses Rocco into quick action in order that Florestan might be killed before Fernando arrives. On the other hand, Beethoven creates sudden spaces or moments of opportunity so that one or more characters can stand outside the action and reflect, meditatively or passionately, as the case may be, on their sentiments. "Mir ist so wunderbar" is a perfect example of this latter device, as is the superb Prisoners' Chorus in act 1, which for a brief moment or two is literally allowed to happen outside Pizarro's dark prison cells.

All of this produces a highly eccentric kind of continuity in *Fidelio*—or perhaps "discontinuity" is a better word for it. If it should happen that a listener first hears *Leonore* and then follows that with a hearing of *Fidelio,* there is every likelihood that the 1814 version of the work will sound disjointed and forced, despite the spoken linking dialogues (retained by Beethoven from *Singspiel*). But *Fidelio* is powerfully effective nonetheless, precisely because the composer has forged a discontinuous style carried forward not by considerations of verisimilitude and realistic psychology, but by leaving those out in favor of the kind of sudden intensifications I have been trying to describe. Still, even with Don Fernando's magical appearance late in the opera, we experience Beethoven's world in most of *Fidelio* as somehow natural and, more important, secular. Leonore and Florestan themselves are ordinary citizens without any apparent hereditary rights. They both have an acute sense of injustice not shared by Rocco, his daughter, or Jaquino. But it is very likely, given what Florestan tells us so sketchily about his past, that he and his wife belong to a better class, albeit one which is less protected and privileged than either Pizarro's or Don Fernando's. Dahlhaus tries to explain the social distinctions in the work with reference to French aesthetic classifications that Beethoven seems to have borrowed from the Encyclopedists (without, alas, much evidence to support this ingenious theory).[8] Thus, Dahlhaus ventures that the early scenes between Rocco, his daughter, Jaquino, and the disguised Fidelio are taken from the *comédie larmoyante*, whereas the interplay between Pizarro, Florestan, and Leonore is based on the *tragédie bourgeoise*; finally, according to Dahlhaus, the tableaus and pathetic scenes that give the opera its unique emotional efficacity are indebted to what Diderot and Lessing considered to be a wider category than the first two, and in fact included them, that of the *genres intermédiaires*. This genre allowed dramatists to assign convincing, affecting, and moving attributes to characters who are not noble or of high civil rank.

Plausible enough, one supposes, but is that the only way to explain *Fidelio*'s extraordinary political and visionary power, given the work's abruptness, its lapses and strange ellipses, as well as its passionate discontinuities? I think not. There seem to me to be two strong and interrelated undercurrents in the work, one political and the other quasi-metaphysical, neither of which has played a prominent role in most analyses of the opera, which begin by accepting its explicit themes of freedom and constancy as defining, if not exhausting, *Fidelio*'s meaning. Part of the difficulty is that Beethoven's only opera ends with the triumphalist tone and canonical authority given it both by the main characteristics of its composer's second-period style and its overt, uncontroversial message. Like other works of this period, *Fidelio* is taken to be internally consistent and in its conclusion accomplishing a complete reconciliation or synthesis of its various elements. Borrowing from Adorno, Rose Rosengard Subotnik formulates the features of Beethoven's second-period style as follows:

> What distinguishes such structures and movements [of this period], in short, is their apparent ability to derive the principle of formal organization not from any outside source but from within themselves, and thus to establish as a reality the musical analogue of the free individual, the "musical subject," which has mastered external constraint and dissent and determined its own destiny. . . . In fact, the recapitulation [or conclusion] seems to confirm the rational irresistibility of the subject's determination to return to itself, since it nearly always seems to emerge as the logical outcome and resolution of what has preceded.[9]

I have been trying to suggest that *Fidelio* is a work riven by various pressures and counterforces, partly the result of its own complicated history as a collaborative, much-fussed-over work whose irregularities of style, disruptive energies, and unstilled, problematic nature were often beyond Beethoven's control. Certainly I think it is wrong to interpret the opera as reconciling all its elements in some miracle ascribed to a creative subject, though naturally enough the work preeminently bears the mark of Beethoven's genius. Steeped though he was in French and

Viennese opera, Beethoven's only attempt to produce one himself was irrevocably stamped with the enormous problems he faced in trying for well over a decade to get it right. *Fidelio* highlights not only its own peculiar features but also those of opera in general, a cultural form that is thoroughly hybrid, mixed, and wonderfully overstated. (Herbert Lindenberger's phrases for opera as "the extravagant art" and "the last remaining refuge of the high style" are perfectly appropriate.)[10] But because opera as spectacle has become so routinized and unthinking, we don't find it in us to do much more than venerate this cultural form and reproduce a whole set of clichés about it, clichés that are no less unthinkingly and uncritically reinforced by modern producers and directors. That there might be something both invisible—fault lines and unresolved antitheses, for instance—and transgressive about most interesting operas eludes the spectator for whom opera is out there, the bigger and more lavish the better. In New York's Metropolitan Opera, for example, there is more applause for a typically overstuffed and under-directed production of a bad Verdi and worse Puccini work than there is understanding of what an appallingly vulgar mess the whole business really is.

We must therefore be prepared to grant that the supposed creative subject behind *Fidelio* is not a unified, but a fractured and only partially coherent thing, surrounded by uncertainties and incapacities, facing problems it cannot resolve and solutions it cannot pull off. *Fidelio*'s political undercurrent is a perfect case in point. Dictatorial tyranny and benevolent redemption operate more or less as equivalents in *Fidelio*. They can be substituted for each other by the miracle, or "myth," as Adorno calls it, of prompt arrival; Pizarro's police and Fernando's trumpet are in fact interchangeable. Florestan's explanation for his plight is that the state has moved against him, but we never learn—nor can we—what sort of state it is. Who are the other prisoners? Are they also unjustly punished intellectuals, or do they include thieves and murderers? All strive for freedom and light, but is it clear that they are all moved by principles (like Florestan) or fidelity to a loved one (like Leonore)? Yes, it is the case, as Maynard Solomon has argued, that the opera moves in act 1 from the above-ground light of Rocco's quarters in the castle to the underground gloom of the prison, and in act 2 from the darkness of Florestan's dungeon to the sunny, liberating atmosphere of the yard;[11] but what can Beethoven do to guarantee that the whole story will not repeat itself—that tyranny will not victimize just people all over again?

The fact is, as Beethoven well knew, that the source of real power in his society lay outside anything that *Fidelio*, as a relatively compressed theatrical work, was able to represent. Beethoven's audience, his patrons in effect, were aristocrats, nor ordinary middle-class citizens. He lived at the heart of an empire during a period of violent change and counterrevolution; the Congress of Vienna, after all, took place while *Fidelio* was performed in 1814 and 1815, and the opera's audience was presumably made up principally of delegates to the gathering. In a seminal article published in 1971, well before his Beethoven biography appeared, Solomon argues that, to the Viennese and Prussian aristocrats who nurtured Beethoven's early career, the

Enlightenment was welcomed not only as the creation of French aristocrats or men like Rousseau who had been adopted by the aristocracy, but it also represented

> a philosophy of duty, service and rationality, in part as a means of avoiding the painful realities of social existence and national fragmentation, in part as the false consciousness of a dying class. . . . And if it was one of the means by which absolutism co-opted the radical intellectual and neutralized the revolutionary mood of its most advanced sections, it simultaneously was one of the means by which absolutism was ultimately destroyed. . . . Separated from the degraded sources [their vast landed estates] of their immense revenues by distance and generations of myopia, the nobility nurtured the arts, and especially music, with a lavishness equalled only by its vast expenditures on food and dress.[12]

Still, for someone like Beethoven there was a "disharmony" between himself and the sources of his patronage, and this, Solomon goes on to say, was "a spur to the breaking of existent molds, of expansion of the means of musical expression." These means in turn supplied new utopian images and in effect permitted the composer to break away from the old style of patronage altogether, to write pieces of his own choosing, not for gifted aristocrats but for professional musicians like himself. If the aristocracy saw in music and elaborate operatic entertainment the possibility of utopian affirmation in spite of war, the revolution and the fading of the old order, then it became possible for a few great musicians to find for themselves a new mode of utopian affirmation—and this, says Solomon daringly, was the sonata form. "The sonata distinguished itself from all other fantasy forms by its containment of its own fantasy-content, its molding of the improvisational, its suppression of the extemporaneous, its rationalization of the irrational. It was with this development that the sonata became a closed, rational, musical system, a 'principle' of composition rather than just another musical form."[13]

The problem with sonata form, however, is that although it furnished a rigorous system of order, tonality, contrast, development, and recapitulation in instrumental music—symphonies, sonatas, string quartets, and so on—it can scarcely serve the same totalizing function in an opera, which is too long and various to be confined in that way. Individual numbers within the opera may employ sonata form, but what commands the work as a whole is the plot, a narrative sequence with its own dynamic of beginning, development, and conclusion. A century after Beethoven, Alban Berg, faced with the same problem in his opera *Wozzeck* (1922), felt that he had to seek a separate principle of musical organization and coherence, for which he devised a remarkably complex series of often archaic forms—classical suite, passacaglia, fugue—to give the opera a sense of "dramatic unity."[14] *Fidelio* belongs to the same tonal and compositional world as the *Eroica* and Fifth Symphony, but Beethoven's problem was that he had to contend with the complexities of characters, scenes, and dramatic tension that required a more flexible system of organizing sound.

What Beethoven retained from his experiences with sonata form is the need for closure, that definitive, conclusive moment in which everything comes to a fulfilling climax, thereby giving a sense of completion and, after a great deal of turbulent struggle, a sense of achieved stability. Hence the crucial status of the final scene—reparation and restoration we might call it—in which punishments and rewards are handed out. The last part of the last chorus is a mighty ensemble led by Leonore and Florestan for all the main characters (except Pizarro) plus the entire chorus. Full of anticipations of the choral movement of the Ninth Symphony, this ensemble concludes with a terrifyingly accented presto section, the last few moments of which settle into an anxiously strident dominant-tonic pattern similar to the last measures of the Fifth Symphony. Ostensibly, the much-repeated words of this section inform us that Leonore cannot be praised too highly, an exultant tribute to her and, by implication, to the new dimension of freedom that seems to have been established thanks to her heroic fidelity.

But there were plenty of indications in preceding scenes that Pizarro's castle is not merely a temporary, makeshift structure, but a dominating feature of the actual world. Even the chorus, which sings away enthusiastically in Fernando's commanding presence, represents townspeople who have lived in close proximity to Pizarro's dungeons and seem never to have heard of him before. And, alas, the genial Rocco reveals himself to have been a collaborator, blaming others for his role as jailer and becoming, in spite of his protestations, Pizarro's virtual accomplice. So the final cadences are in effect much more provisional than they sound—a temporary union of Beethoven's romantic and utopian impulses with the sordid world he and his librettists have been representing throughout the opera. And then there is the silence that simply confirms the precariousness of the affirmative cadence, which cannot be extended beyond the last C major chord. Solomon puts it well, and though he only mentions *Fidelio* in passing, I think his remarks apply well to that work, too:

> In Beethoven, no affirmation is complete: the finale of the *Eroica* Symphony is prelude to the struggles of the Fifth; the brittle affirmations of the Fifth's finale in turn do not result in harmony or resolution. There are no ultimate reconciliations in Beethoven; there are a series of Utopian reconfirmations, but all are conditional, one-sided, temporary. Each work in Beethoven's total output is part of a larger entity, and each affirmation, each happy ending, looks forward to a new struggle, to further agonies of introspection, to Winter, death and towards a new victorious conclusion. . . . The works are a perpetual cycle of struggle, death and rebirth. Each work looks both backward and forward—Janus-like—for within the work, the happy ending acknowledges the pain which preceded it.[15]

This brings us to the metaphysical current in *Fidelio*. It derives from an extended cultural pattern during this period, well described by M. H. Abrams in his book *Natural Supernaturalism*. The age of the French Revolution is one of "apocalyptic expectation," which impresses a whole generation of poets, philosophers, as well as Beethoven himself. Yet most of them lose "confidence in a millennium brought about by means of violent revolution," though "they did not abandon the form of their earlier vision. In many important philosophers and poets, Romantic thinking and imagination remained apocalyptic thinking and imagination, though with varied changes in explicit content."[16] In *Fidelio,* as well as in works like the Ninth Symphony, Beethoven is very much of this disenchanted yet still apocalyptic cast of mind; one finds in those works the kind of reconstituted theology that Abrams speaks about, albeit in a radically problematic musical and dramatic form that, almost in spite of itself, highlights a lack of confidence in millennial change while retaining aspects of its enthusiastic sense of triumph.

It would seem that *Fidelio*'s internal wrestling with its own past, trying to shed its earthbound early versions and its own dramatic setting in the actual with an intensely elevated lunge at utopian brotherhood, points forward to Beethoven's so-called late period style and to the torments of his last years. He never stopped looking for another opera libretto to set, but because of his deafness and the anomalies of his fame and isolation he retreated more and more into the abstruse style announced in 1816 by Opus 101, the A major Piano Sonata, and in 1817–1818 by Opus 106, the *Hammerklavier* Sonata. What in *Fidelio*'s last scene is left implicitly unarticulated beneath the resounding final C major chords is uncovered once and for all in the late style where, as Adorno has said, Beethoven attempts no reconciliation between sections: "The caesuras, the sudden discontinuities that more than anything else characterize the very late Beethoven, are those moments of breaking away; the work is silent at the instant when it is left behind, and turns its emptiness outward." According to Adorno, Beethoven's late style "sets the mere phrase as a monument to what has been, marking a subjectivity turned to stone."[17] The uniqueness of *Fidelio* is that it arises, so to speak, in the heroic element of his middle period, but through Beethoven's unstinting efforts it ends up as precursor and announcement of the final works. No final synthesis here, but rather testimony to what Adorno calls Beethoven's "power of dissociation": his ability to tear the works "apart in time, in order, perhaps, to preserve them for the eternal."[18]

Chapter Three

LES TROYENS AND THE OBLIGATION TO EMPIRE

FULL OF EXTRAVAGANT PASSIONS and the most extraordinary energies and counterenergies, Hector Berlioz's works still do not occupy the honored place in music that I think they clearly deserve. "Eccentricity" is the first word that leaps to mind—eccentricity and a certain stubborn persistence throughout his life for somehow being outside his period and place, at the same time that no one more than Berlioz participated in both indefatigably as composer, conductor, critic, journalist, and all-around observer. Yes, he was a charter member of what Jacques Barzun in his monumental study of the man and his time called "the romantic century," but he was also forever having difficulty getting the right kind of attention and respect in Paris, where he lived for five decades.[1] Suffice it to say, as an indication of what he had to go through—even when great musicians like Liszt, Schumann, and Chopin publicly celebrated his music and talent, and when his fame in Germany, England, and Russia was very widespread—that his greatest and culminating work, *Les Troyens*, composed between 1856 and 1858, could not be performed in its entirety in Paris during his lifetime. The most that could be managed in 1863 at the Théâtre Lyrique (not the Opéra) was a three-act abridgement in which nearly everything went wrong. The first complete performance of the work took place in Germany in 1890 (Berlioz died in 1869), and, so far as I know, Paris has never witnessed a complete and uncut performance of what is arguably the greatest French opera ever written.[2]

What Berlioz had to say about Beethoven's *Fidelio* surely applies much more to *Les Troyens*:

> It belongs to that strong race of maligned works drenched in the most inconceivable prejudices, and the most manifest lies; but its vitality is so great nothing can prevail against it. They are like vigorous beeches, born amidst rocks and ruins, who end by splitting the rocks and piercing the rubble, and finally rising proud and verdant, all the more solidly implanted because of the obstacles they had to conquer in order to emerge; while willows growing without trouble along the river bank, fall into its bed, and die forgotten.[3]

Despite the overall confidence in this passage, a defensive note that probably applies to Berlioz himself is hard to ignore. Perhaps this was the result of fighting for recognition and the right to compose as he saw fit, first with his family, who wanted their brilliant son to be a doctor like his father and abhorred his wish to be a musician, then with a whole range of authorities, who saw in Berlioz a threat to their way of doing things. Even today among the most perceptively refined critics there is a strangely grudging, occasionally even unpleasant, tone when Berlioz is discussed. It seems that his greatness can only be conceded when it is whittled down to something vaguely contemptible or funny, like his obsession with enormous orchestras or the fact that alone among the major nineteenth-century composers he never really learned how to play the piano, being a flutist and guitarist instead. Charles Rosen, normally an acutely sympathetic listener and analyst, is patronizingly snide about Berlioz's unorthodox harmonic and aesthetic ideas, arguing that "it is not Berlioz's oddity but his normality, his ordinariness, that makes him great." Specifically with regard to *Les Troyens*, Rosen describes the opera as "the musical equivalent of the *grandes machines* that the so-called *pompiers* displayed at the midcentury salons—a pretentious historical costume drama, life-size and imperturbably honest."[4] Yet Rosen is not as offensive to Berlioz as Felix Mendelssohn was, but who is nonetheless quoted by Rosen at the outset: "With all his efforts to go stark mad [Berlioz] never once succeeds."[5]

More helpful than Rosen is Pierre Boulez, who accounts for Berlioz as anomaly, for the failure of his music to be "absorbed" and "become an integral part of tradition."[6] Boulez continues, noting that no other great composer of the time was as personal as Berlioz:

> Everything helped to make Berlioz a predestined victim of the imaginary. His compositions both transcend and fall short of the conventions; it is only with great difficulty that

> they can finally be inserted into the customary framework of the theatre or the concert. They overrate the latter and underrate the former. The limitations inherent in a social form of transmission have scarcely any *raison d'être* or any logic; we are fully aware of their artificial character, which restricts the imaginary and does not allow it to find expression in an immaterial, fluid dimension. All the circumstances that make the concert and the theatre what they are seem too restricting to [Berlioz's] form of the imaginary; they suppress, to a large extent, its reason for existing.[7]

This is a provocative way of putting it: how someone whose transcendental passions for Beethoven, Shakespeare, and Virgil could not be accommodated easily into the conventions of the concert hall or opera house. And Boulez is right to the degree that we sometimes tend to see only the gigantism in Berlioz, or the way in which his ideas and images spill out beyond the walls. Take as a perfect example the elaborate pantomime that is supposed to accompany the dazzling "Royal Hunt and Storm" music that opens act 4 of *Les Troyens*. Naiads, Tyrian horsemen, dogs, Dido dressed as the huntress Diana, satyrs and sylvans, fauns; pools and streams that become torrents and waterfalls; thunder and lightning, which destroys a tree—Berlioz *sees* all these things in his mind's eye, although, of course, no opera house in the 1850s could possibly have even begun to accommodate such a spectacle. Most often, therefore, such scenes get cut, the music either not played at all or transformed into a mystifying prelude to the dramatic action that follows.

For sheer grandeur of scale, conscious elevation of style, and audacity of conception, *Les Troyens* is *Der Ring des Nibelungen*'s only nineteenth-century competitor. Yet whereas Wagner lived to see his tetralogy staged and canonized in his own specially built opera house in Bayreuth, Berlioz saw only the second half of his two-part adaptation from books 1, 2, and 4 of Virgil's *Aeneid* realized. And, over its twenty-one performances in 1863, this realization became a more and more shoddy, truncated, badly sung condensation that gave little idea to its dwindling public of what the work was all about. French audiences were the least prepared to accept innovation in Europe; the musical establishment and institutions were by and large more conventional, stuffy, and maliciously competitive than elsewhere.

Despite the fact that Berlioz was a visionary cosmopolitan more spiritually at home with Beethoven and Gluck than with many French composers—he was, by the way, astonishingly uninformed about the classical tradition (i.e., Bach, Handel, Haydn, and Mozart), and he was one of the only major nineteenth-century composers not to have been nourished on Bach's *Well-Tempered Clavier*—he was also profoundly immersed in Parisian cultural and governmental politics as well as influenced by French theatrical currents of the time. The rhetoric and vocabulary of *Les Troyens* are nineteenth-century romantic transformations of seventeenth-century classical drama and eighteenth-century neoclassicism; so, too, are its depictions of Cassandra and Dido, the opera's two magnificent mezzo-soprano heroines, who divide the work between them. *Les Troyens* is emphatically a grand opera, a principally Parisian phenomenon. Berlioz's innovative ideas about the genre are indebted not only to Meyerbeer, Spontini, Rossini, and Auber but also to Gluck (a German), whose operas were originally intended for and staged in Paris; Berlioz himself mounted a celebrated production of Gluck's *Orfeo* in 1859. And, I would argue, Berlioz's daring theatrical imagination used *Les Troyens* as an artistic vehicle for embodying in music and drama the contemporary expansion of the French empire in North Africa, which is where the second half of the work (acts 3, 4, and 5) is set, in ancient Carthage.

In trying to make more detailed sense of *Les Troyens,* we should first recall that Paris opera—unlike Viennese opera at the time of *Così fan tutte* and *Fidelio*—was an intensely, indeed feverishly political, institution. Between 1830 and 1870, the choice of opera, frequency of presentation, and style of production were subject first of all to the pressures of the government, for whom questions of patriotism, democracy (participatory or not), and legitimacy were of the utmost importance in the attempt to regulate public life during crises such as the 1830 and 1848 upheavals. By order of Emperor Louis-Napoléon Bonaparte in 1854, shortly before Berlioz began work on *Les Troyens*, the Opéra was no longer run by independent entrepreneurs (among them Berlioz himself) but came under the control of the Ministre d'État et de la Maison de l'Empereur. As a form that evolved from about 1830 on, French grand opera, with its immense crowd scenes, great length, and opulent production, was treated as an important factor in political life dominated not only by the court and government but also by boulevardiers, workers, insurgents, and intellectuals. Above all, opera was somehow to contain and perhaps even neutralize conflicts during an extremely volatile period so that audiences could feel their interests represented, enacted, and reconciled for the general good of France. During the 1840s, two major ingredients of grand opera thus emerged: the need to inculcate a general feeling of the *patrimoine nationale*—even to the extent of provoking audiences to join in patriotic songs during the opera's final scenes—and the need to reflect a sense of France's own current grandeur.

Although he is rarely performed today, Giacomo Meyerbeer interposes himself as a major figure at this point. Both Wagner and Berlioz were often extremely worked up at his preeminence as a composer of grand opera during this time, in particular because he was so clever at successfully adapting his grandiose historical works to the political necessities of a given moment. Given the fact that in 1861 Wagner's *Tannhäuser* was a famous Paris fiasco, and that *Les Troyens* never even made it on to the Opéra's boards, the two men had good reason both to envy and grudgingly admire Meyerbeer's decades-long success. In the book *The Nation's Image*, Jane Fulcher gives an excellent analysis of Meyerbeer's methods and reputation.[8] She argues that, through representing the 1572 St. Bartholomew's Day Massacre in his 1836 opera *Les Huguenots*, Meyerbeer brought forward the distant past by constructing an *actualité* that directly touched a contemporary audience. By skillful, not to say ingenious, dodges he skirted censorship laws that protected the monarchy, which took offence at his opera anyway but was made to seem ridiculous in the contentious press maelstrom that ensued.[9] According to Fulcher, Berlioz "was both 'impressed and repelled' by

Meyerbeer's 'snakelike flexibility,' and yet he did still admire *Les Huguenots*. For him, as he expressed it in a letter to his sister in 1836, *Les Huguenots* was no less an *'encyclopédie musicale.'* He recognized immediately . . . that it was 'a vast canvas richly embroidered,' outstanding in 'its sweep and control of detail.' "[10] Meyerbeer's minutely constructed concerted numbers, in which music whipped up choruses, historical personages, and dancers into massive climaxes that grew out of intimate scenes or solo arias, became a model for *Les Troyens*, even though Berlioz was a good deal more subtle and elevated in the musical and political effects than Meyerbeer.

All of the commentaries on *Les Troyens* that I have read—many of them, especially those by Julian Rushton, Hugh MacDonald, and D. Kern Holoman, extremely valuable—suppose that the opera is somehow outside the contested political and cultural ground fought over by other operatic composers of the time.[11] I think this is wrong. An indefatigable journalist, man about town, and entrepreneur, Berlioz could not have been untouched by the crosscurrents of his time, not the least of which was the debate over France itself, its glory, its national patrimony, and its worldwide destiny. Rather than directly engaging these matters, Berlioz's coup in *Les Troyens* was to outbid all his competitors (including Meyerbeer) by harnessing his passion for Virgil to a much-subdivided plot that takes audiences back to France's Latin origins in the Roman Empire. As early as the thirteenth century, the medieval epics of antiquity had been a lively topic; seventeenth-century authors like Pierre Corneille returned to it in plays like *Horace* (1640), and, of course, the French Revolution and Napoleon (an early hero of Berlioz) revived Roman customs and ambitions, especially in their conquest of the East, in styles and modes with which Berlioz grew up. Thus, from its audacious opening pages, which for sixty-six measures employ no strings and rely totally on brasses and woodwinds, *Les Troyens* communicates a kind of aural originality that lifts it out of the habitual grand opera world into an exotic eastern world, doubly familiar as classic and oriental.

To this opening scene, with its gigantic wooden horse, its swirling crowds, and its single tragic figure of Cassandra, Berlioz adds the chromatic "ah" of the chorus that unexpectedly inflects his score with a destabilizing strangeness, which will build through acts 1 and 2 into the mass quasi-orientalist suicide scene of Cassandra and her female companions. In this Berlioz was manifestly influenced by Eugène Delacroix's celebrated painting *The Death of Sardanapalus* (1827), whose blazing color and carefully composed scene of suicidal albeit fleshly abandon was not only emulated but exceeded by Berlioz in that final scene of act 2. What we watch beforehand is a carefully prepared, mountingly ironic tension between the celebrating Trojans on the one hand, who are overjoyed at a respite from ten years of Greek attacks and who believe that the wooden horse is meant as an offering to the gods, and on the other hand Cassandra, who in the course of two acts first uselessly warns and then dramatically separates herself from her fiancé, her family, and all but a small number of the unaware Trojans. Possessed with a keen, angry sense of the disaster to be visited on her city, she stands alone and resolute throughout the rituals, dances, and celebrations all around her; meanwhile, Berlioz increases the exoticism and thereby the distance separating us from the Trojans.

Deliberately monumental and grand in the effects he tries to achieve, Berlioz composes scenes in what appear to be fiery bursts, and he is never held in by cautious reliance on a logical or even plausible plot. Yet his plans, directions, and notations are extremely precise, disproving all the worn clichés about romanticism as vague and turgidly grandiose. Everything seems to have been calculated to achieve the maximum in expressivity, melancholy, and a cumulative (if understated) political statement, at the same time that he had no illusions that his directions were going to be followed. In 1857, he wrote to his sister Adèle prophetically that of a dozen specific effects he planned for a given section of *Les Troyens* he knew that opera houses would give him at most two or three.[12]

Berlioz's special genius—constantly at work in *Les Troyens*—is for division and subdivision, followed by combination and then synthesis, almost in the Hegelian sense. What carries this forward is a general attitude toward history, which, concurrently with Berlioz's compositions, appears in the work of historian Jules Michelet, for example, where the history of France is seen to be creating itself organically and emerging out of feudalism toward modernity. The incessant counterpoint between Cassandra and the Trojan chorus, Aeneas's narrative of the death of Laocoön, the offstage attack of the Greeks: all these culminate not only in the mass suicide of Cassandra and her followers but also in their announcement as they die that Italy is where Aeneas, his men, and Priam's treasures are providentially going to end up. Berlioz's technique is to anchor this conception in the Trojan March, first heard at the end of act 1, as a naively triumphant anthem before the Greeks begin their assault, and then again at crucial junctures in the three Carthaginian acts, where it is variously transformed to suit the occasion.

After hearing the Trojan March at the end of act 1, Cassandra returns in act 2 as if condemned to witness and then narrate the fall of Troy and Aeneas's escape with his men and the treasure. In what I think is the most thrilling ensemble scene in nineteenth-century opera—the finale to the collapse of Troy as experienced by Cassandra and the chorus of Trojan women—she strikes an authentically tragic, almost demonic note: she provokes the chorus of women into mass suicide as an alternative to Greek servitude. She first enjoins the other women to face their stark fate if they would simply give up to the rampaging Greeks: "Mais vous, colombes effarées, / Pouvez-vous consentir / A l'horrible esclavage? / Et voudrez-vous subir, / Vierges, femmes déshonorées, / La loi brutale des vainqueurs?" (But you, frightened doves, can you consent to horrible slavery? And will you submit, dishonored maidens and women, to the brutal law of the conquerors?). The group then subdivides into those who are unwilling to die (who leave) and those who choose death with Cassandra. In the long climax that follows, Berlioz's use of the orchestra to produce a quintessential moment of operatic transcendence is astonishing. His blazingly taut conception of the scene—which includes the mezzo soloist, the main chorus, the small chorus of timorous women, a Greek captain looking for the Trojan treasure, and a chorus of Greek soldiers bursting on the scene as Cassandra plunges a sword into her belly—makes the orchestra by turns menacing, jubilant, hysterical, and triumphant. Harps, agitated triple time clarinets, strings, woodwinds, tympani, and trumpets move forward with shattering effect, the whole culminating in the great D flat chords to the chorus's cries of "Italie."

Berlioz's intention here and at several points in the opera is to keep reminding his audience by such moments of transcendence that, despite the Trojan travails, a new Troy will be created in Italy—from which, of course, will come the Roman Empire and its contemporary heir, the French. This proleptic triumphalism is more insistent a motif in *Les Troyens* than it is in the early books of the *Aeneid*. True, Berlioz's Virgilian passion, as he called it, was perhaps the dominating aesthetic idea in his life, but it received added consolidation from his no less consistent admiration for French imperial expansion. Napoleon pioneered the first great successes of the empire with his celebrated Egyptian campaign in 1798. In 1830, France occupied Algeria, and for decades thereafter it was engaged both in putting down one rebellion after another by decimating the local population and in gradually incorporating the territory into its imperial system by filling it with hundreds of thousands of colonists. Morocco was attacked in 1844; Guinea was made into a protectorate in 1849. All of this was part of Berlioz's world, not least his extraordinary admiration for Bonaparte and his heirs; indeed, one of his lesser compositions was an *Emperor* Cantata (1854) for Napoleon III. Jacques Barzun is right to suggest that Berlioz's political ideas were not really codified as between democracy or aristocracy, but, as others have noted, there is nothing in Berlioz to suggest an interest in democracy.[13]

Moreover, his first composition was based on Charles Hubert Millevoye's poem "The Arab Mourning His Steed," and from beginning to end Berlioz was, like so many of his contemporaries (Hugo, Chateaubriand, Delacroix), fascinated with the Orient. Barzun also speculates that Berlioz's Italian journey in the early 1830s informs many of his greatest works, including *Les Troyens*, not only because it infused him with that sunny dash and romance we find in Goethe and Stendhal, but also because Italy was the site of Europe's first southern empire.[14]

I do not want to suggest that Berlioz was an imperialist in a chauvinistically reductive sense, any more than I want to argue that *Les Troyens* is a crudely ideological opera. Nevertheless, I believe that it is incomprehensible as a great work of art without some account of the heady grandeur it shares both with Virgil as the poet of empire and with the imperial France in and for which it was written. In act 3 of the opera, Carthage's queen Dido is at first a contented, if somewhat emotionally scarred, North African monarch who has come from Tyre on the Lebanese coast after her husband's death and has established herself in a new country. In stark contrast to the fall of Troy in the immediately preceding act, Dido is initially seen languidly surveying her subjects, her military triumphs, and her lush fields. From the moment that Aeneas and the wandering Trojans enter her life, however, she experiences great passion and an ever-growing sorrow. After a sublimely beautiful duet with Aeneas, "Nuit d'ivresse"—based not on Virgil but on some lines from Shakespeare's *The Merchant of Venice* (1598)—her happiness is abruptly ended when, without any warning, Aeneas is summoned back to his men to resume his imperial mission to Italy.

Berlioz intersperses the love scenes with ballets and vignettes of Trojan sentinels, comparing the pleasures of Carthaginian women with the rigors of sea life, or with anxious exchanges between Dido and her sister Anna. The overall theme is the obligation to serve the idea of imperial destiny, no matter the terrible human costs, which, I think, even Berlioz realized were not so easy to slough off.

It is clear that here, as in the previous Troy section of the opera, Berlioz is mostly concerned with the tragedies of royalty, of great historical personages, of national destiny. But even more than the somewhat one-dimensional Aeneas, Dido is required to go back and forth between her official and private selves. It is a less taxing role than Cassandra's, which is so full of fiery—not to say cataclysmic—outbursts addressed either to the gods or to the whole of Troy, and Dido is allowed a wider range of expression. Act 3 introduces us to Dido, her people, and her troubling history as a fugitive widow from the Lebanese coast; midway through the act, the fugitive Trojans appear, are welcomed by her, and are immediately (and willingly) involved in defending Carthage from a threatening African tribe. All of this is carefully rendered by Berlioz and his phenomenal ability to subdivide and distinguish between the citizens of Tyre, Greece, Carthage, Troy, the African desert, and the ever-present "Italie," and to link all of this to music adequate to their dramatic representation. Unlike Wagner, he does not cover his tracks with long theoretical or historical disquisitions on art, his own music, and the destiny of his people, but instead relies on the direct sensuous power of music to move and, indeed, persuade his audiences into assent. Berlioz is very frank about this.

In his book *Musical Travels in Germany and Italy* (1844), he dismisses the music of the ancients in order to elevate the "power"—a word he often uses—of modern music. "Music," he says, is "the art of moving intelligent human beings, endowed with special, well-trained organs by means of combinations of sounds. . . . Simply by glancing around it would be easy to cite incontrovertible facts in favor of the power of our own music—facts whose worth would at least equal that of the doubtful anecdotes of ancient historians."[15]

We know from his letters that he went from composing act 1 directly to act 4, the most subtle and affectingly lyrical of all the acts of the opera. In a letter to Adèle of February 25, 1857, he called it "the act of tenderness, of love, of fêtes and hunts, and the starlit African night," which of course he had never seen.[16] Berlioz in any case was not beyond reveling in the beauties of what he had written, often complimenting himself on the beauty of his score and finding in his concentrated work on the opera an "extraordinary pleasure," as he wrote to Liszt's friend Princess Sayn-Wittgenstein on November 30, 1857. In the same letter, he said that he experienced "a real and deep happiness in digging out and fashioning and fitting up this great Robinson Crusoe's canoe which I shan't be able to launch unless the sea itself comes for it."[17] Typically, he leads up to the Shakespearean duet between Dido and Aeneas by parceling out the action into a series of numbers—a quintet, then a septet, then a duet—whose aim is to slow down, extend, and deepen time, so much so that public and official business is simply crowded out. Here, to use Pierre Boulez's phrase for Berlioz's besetting tendency, he almost gets lost in an imaginary realm of pure, ecstatic stillness.[18] Dido sings a line of which Berlioz was particularly fond—"Tout conspire / A vaincre mes remords et mon cœur est absous" (Everything conspires to overcome my remorse and absolve my heart)—while Aeneas's son Ascanius leans over, looking like a statute of Eros, as Berlioz's stage directions specify. This is the moment that prepares Dido and Aeneas to sing their sublime G flat duet "Nuit d'ivresse et d'extase infinie" (Night of intoxication and infinite ecstasy). The placidity of this duet is sustained by a rocking barcarolle-like rhythm and an essentially simple harmonic structure clustered around the tonic. Yet there are occasional flirtations with a more chromatic harmony as well as some almost imperceptible syncopations in the music's otherwise exaggeratedly calm surface. Toward the end of the piece, a few rising scales in the bass bring to mind Cassandra's music in act 1; only in the final measures, just after Berlioz has brilliantly staved off a conclusion by producing a gentle modulation to D major, it becomes apparent that the call to imperial obligation has once more intruded itself on the privacy of Aeneas's life. Mercury suddenly appears on a moonbeam and sings out "Italie" three times, as act 4 is concluded on three ominous E minor chords.

Although the final act actually begins with a pair of deliberately distracting, low-key pieces, its real burden is announced by Aeneas's sudden wish to leave Dido and head north to Italy. One feels no doubt that he is genuinely torn between his real love for Dido and the injunction to get back to the business of establishing a new empire. But what becomes evident at this late point in the opera is how every call to Italy that dots the score, beginning with Cassandra's, emanates from a divinely privileged and thus distinctly nonhuman agency—Cassandra herself being endowed against her will with the gift of prophecy. Thus Aeneas is successively spurred on by the ghosts of Priam, Hector, Cassandra, and her lover Chorèbe. Clearly Berlioz wants to represent the founding of the Roman Empire as more authoritatively and transcendentally fueled than so relatively trivial a force as Aeneas's will or Trojan skill at arms. And so he sets the call to Italy at a distinct remove from the historical foreground of the action, something outside time and hidden from ordinary perception, like an unconscious imperative that bends individuals and collectivities to a deeply immanent force.

Herbert Lindenberger is right to remark that "the great nineteenth-century operas retain only the most tenuous possible relationship to what our common sense considers historical truth." And regarding *Les Troyens*, he states that the public ceremonial character of the work magnifies the conflict of Troy and Carthage "so that we are allowed to feel the whole weight of historical process as only a nineteenth-century imagination could have conceived it."[19] No less just is Julian Rushton, who says that Berlioz always invented rather than used already existing genres, despite the great influence on him of Gluck and Spontini. Thus, in *Les Troyens*, "he eliminates anything recalcitrant to musical elaboration, minimizes declamation, and elaborates elements in a dramatic scheme suggestive of musical expansion: lyricism, passionate confrontation, ritual."[20] Yet neither of these characterizations goes far enough, and they do not take into account the particular contemporary nature of the history and expansion that are the driving forces of *Les Troyens*—namely, conquest and empire. For, in a very meaningful way, it is a work not just about war, but about war and conquest against inferior others, who are identified either as people who fight for the sake of profit—these are the Greeks in acts 1 and 2—or people like the Carthaginians, whose fate Dido embodies, who are sedentary agriculturalists, traders, and pleasure seekers without a real sense of national purpose.

In the first two Carthaginian acts (3 and 4) this is made abundantly clear in Dido's tribute to her land and people as prosperous, successful planters and merchants. She gives Aeneas and his men a great deal of luxurious pleasure—which is why the two Trojan sentries at the beginning of act 5 complain about leaving Carthage—complete with dancing oriental "almahs" and Nubian slaves, the former number sounding like music by Jacques Offenbach and the latter like the silliest golliwog stereotypes of the sort that Debussy would later exploit. But partly because of this epicene comfort, she and her people are incapable of perceiving, much less understanding, the stern tasks imposed on a chosen people by history. To create this heedless sense in Dido and Carthage, Berlioz tapped the same lode exploited by Gustave Flaubert in his Egyptian travel diaries (1850), and later in *Salammbô* (1862) and some of the imagery in *L'Education sentimentale* (1869), and in the contemporary work of Théophile Gautier and Maxime du Camp. Oriental women are sensual, largely unthinking creatures who are devoted to lovemaking and, in Dido's case, fatally available to strong male suitors. But Berlioz also subordinated this theme to the political designs of a man like Aeneas who is in the grip of historical forces he can only assent to. Enjoyment is spectacle and a kind of static nondevelopment, which in retrospect the great love duet at the end of act 4 seems both musically and historically to represent.

On the other hand, the various calls to empire that animate Aeneas throughout the opera all come from an out-of-the-ordinary, normally inaccessible source or place. Except for Cassandra and her companions (who are literally in extremis when they sing their prophecy), Berlioz is careful to represent Aeneas's imperial obligations to keep moving on toward Italy as out of history in some way, unconscious perhaps (as when he is addressed by ghosts in his sleep), above all as something he cannot in the end question or engage with except by obedient compliance. And because he must along the way abandon a magnificent, authentically regal woman who loves him unconditionally, Aeneas emerges as no mere adventurer or heartless conquistador; for in giving up Dido, he also relinquishes Carthage, which out of her boundless love she has effectively ceded to him. To establish a truly grand and durable empire, the once-destitute Trojans who arrived in Carthage as tattered shipwrecks must do more giving up than holding on. There is a stern askesis required of Aeneas, which he must ruefully accept, even though he is still wholly in love with Dido and the ambiance of lush enjoyment and repose that being with her stands for. Empire is not only a way of life, but also a calling that cannot be served by mere self-enrichment or acquisition; it requires the continuity and system of institutions, undeterred strength and sustained purpose, moral elevation above satisfaction and appetite. But there is a startlingly modern quality to it as Berlioz represents the authority of the idea itself as it would activate thousands of colonial servants during the remainder of the nineteenth century. Anticipating Joseph Conrad, Berlioz isolates the reminders of imperial obligation in such a way as to exact service and loyalty on the one hand, and on the other hand, "not too much looking into it."[21]

Dido's anger at being abandoned in act 5 quickly reduces itself to a condition that combines passionate hatred and a beautifully rendered, elaborate, but finally impotent fulmination, replete with curses, ritual imprecations, and forecasts of future vengeance against Rome via Hannibal. In one of the great poetic images of the work, Dido sings: "Je vais mourir / Dans ma douleur immense submergée / Et mourir non vengée" (I will die, submerged in my intense grief—and I will die unavenged). To this she adds her poignant, Shakespearean farewell with its final allusion to *Othello*: "Adieu, beau ciel d'Afrique, astres que j'admirai / Aux nuits d'ivresse et d'extase infinie; / Je ne vous verrai plus, ma carrière est finie" (Farewell, beautiful African sky, stars that I admired, farewell to nights of intoxication and infinite ecstasy, I will see you no more, my journey has ended). Berlioz balances her ceremonial suicide against Cassandra's in act 2, the difference being that the Trojan princess prophesies a fulfilled imperial greatness, whereas Dido's attempt to sketch a heroic destiny for her people on the African land ("sur la terre africaine") will only lead to Carthage's destruction.

Against the background of the French pacification campaign in North Africa under Marshal Bugeaud, whose aim was *la conquête totale* during the 1840s, Dido's desolation in Carthage must have aroused some recollection of the French (or, in the generic sense, Latin) role in the place. And, although Aeneas leaves for Italy, we cannot but feel that his antithetical conquest of and love for Dido were both real and lasting. In any event, out of the encounter between France and Algeria, between Aeneas and Dido, a powerful hate is born. In a letter of December 1, 1846, Alexis de Tocqueville describes his impressions of this unequivocally. After first characterizing the local population as being in a state of complete subjugation and capitulation, he observes:

> I do not think that from now till the next harvest we have any insurrection to fear. There is a state of calm. But it is not peace. The hatred that reigns between the two races, especially in those regions which have just been agitated by war, is very pitiful to see; contempt and anger fill the hearts of our officers and one can clearly see that in their eyes the Arabs are like discontented beasts. The death of each one of them seems for our officers to be a good thing.[22]

Yet Berlioz's dramatic and musical gifts go beyond this criminal stalemate without in any way reconciling the deep opposition, the unhealable rift, between Dido and Aeneas, between imperialism and its victims. The final scene of *Les Troyens* reveals Dido in her death throes; represented behind her we see the Roman Capitol, with the word "Rome" emblazoned on its pediment. Military legions as well as a court of poets and artists surround an unnamed emperor. All of this is unseen by the Carthaginians, standing loyally by the dying Dido, whose last words are "Rome . . . Rome . . . immortelle." Once again the

Trojan (now Roman) March is heard, to which in response Dido's retainers sing discordantly: "Haine éternelle à la race d'Énée" (Eternal hatred to the race of Aeneas). The effect of their dissonant A flat against the March's B flat produces an electrifying theatrical effect. But even the Carthaginians are absorbed by the March, resolved into the triumphal chords that bring down the curtain, as if to suggest that imperial Rome presses on regardless. The true result of this scene, however, is to show that the expense of Aeneas's greatness can never be shed or abolished so long as it is sustained by either memory or art. Far from simply subordinating Dido's experience to the imperial quest, it is her presence on stage that Berlioz leaves us with even as he lifts the imperial image to the status of deferred, distant realization. He had hoped that Napoleon III would first read the manuscript and then attend a performance of *Les Troyens*, but, since the emperor did neither one nor the other, it was just as well for Berlioz's fortunes that he did not. Surely the final scene of the opera, far from being merely academic or nationalistic, impresses the audience with a powerfully affecting image of a supremely grieving woman whose death symbolizes a sense of waste and sorrow implanted forever at the heart of transcendently victorious success.

Chapter Four

CREATION AND COHERENCE IN *DIE MEISTERSINGER*

WAGNER IS perhaps the most difficult of all composers to speak or write about. His works, life, and reputation are now surrounded with so much commentary, scholarship, analysis, and invective that a dispassionate attempt to say something more about him is extremely hard. But what is remarkable is the recent resurgence of interest in the works on the part of the nonspecialist general public. New York's Metropolitan Opera now regularly schedules performances of *Der Ring des Nibelungen*, and, with discouraging regularity for people who want to attend the cycles, they are immediately sold out. Despite the fact that staging works like *Der Ring des Nibelungen*, or even *Parsifal*, *Tristan und Isolde*, and *Die Meistersinger von Nürnberg* is a tremendously costly and difficult undertaking, new Wagner productions (and, of course, debates about them) spring up in many different places. Various avant-garde productions such as the Richard Jones *Ring* at Covent Garden (1994), David Hockney's

Los Angeles *Tristan* (1987), or the Harry Kupfer *Ring* at the Berlin Staatsoper (1996) suggest that the energy driving directors, musicians, and audiences to discover new aspects of Wagner's astonishingly fertile and demanding art is as robust as ever, perhaps even more so now.

There is something about Wagner that imprints itself on the mind in a unique way, quite unlike any other musical encounter. I have never forgotten one old 78 rpm, rather haphazardly included in my family's record collection as I was growing up in Cairo. On one side of the record was "Hagen's Call," on the other "Hagen's Watch," both of them sung in English by Norman Allin, whose large dark voice totally captivated me, even though the two extracts were only minutes long and at the time I had little idea what *The Twilight of the Gods* (and Wagner, for that matter) were all about. The remote and unfamiliar, threatening and savage quality of the music held me in its grip. I saw my first Wagner opera, *Lohengrin*, sung in Italian during the regular winter season of the Cairo Opera, but that, alas, had a negative, soporific effect on me; there was a lot of standing around, as I recall, and there was not much interest in the work communicated to the audience desultorily by the mostly indifferent and largely inappropriate cast. Yet even when I came to the United States during the 1950s, Wagner's operas were not that easily seen. During my university years I attended performances at New York's Metropolitan and City Opera, but never one of Wagner's, the reason being that the Met's general manager, Rudolf Bing, was reportedly more interested in developing the Italian repertory and simply avoided the *Ring*, though perhaps some of Wagner's earlier works were given from time to time. At university I took a Wagner seminar, but there, too, we were limited to a few recorded extracts and to playing scores on the piano; no complete *Ring* recording existed until Georg Solti's version was issued in the 1960s. I can therefore remember with the most vivid clarity my first visit to Bayreuth in 1958, and even more the opening measures of *Das Rheingold* welling up slowly from the hidden orchestra in the Festspielhaus. I had never heard them played by an orchestra before; the extraordinary enchantment and subtle power of the music held me in its spell in a way I have never again experienced.

Certainly for my generation the possibility of seeing and hearing Wagner afresh was enabled by the postwar Bayreuth productions of Wieland and Wolfgang Wagner. Gone were all the bearskins and helmets, the shaggy forests and primitive huts; what was left instead was a great emphasis on stylized, almost immobilized movement on the part of the singers, abstract stage sets that used mostly lighting and one or two simple props in the *Ring* (an enormous disc, for instance, that could be raised, tilted, divided in two as the action warranted) to suggest an indeterminate world of distant, albeit theatrical, action, very far removed from the distinctly Germanic world of earlier productions. Wagner, one surmised, was to be scrubbed clean of his historical encumbrances, delivered to a postwar Germany attempting to reconstruct itself with a carefully vetted image of a universalized and ahistorical Wagner. The 1956 Bayreuth production of *Die Meistersinger*—given that, much more than the *Ring*, the only comic opera that Wagner wrote is an ensemble work with a prominent role for the chorus—was even more startlingly abstract, with no reference made in the rather barren setting to historical Nuremberg, which the composer was at great pains to describe in his instructions for producing the work. In any event, the Wagner brothers' boldness cleared the way for subsequent departures from the dutiful naturalism that had been de rigueur for prewar Wagner productions at the Bayreuth Festspielhaus. Patrice Chéreau's centenary *Ring* (1976), which was conducted by Pierre Boulez with a paradigmatic clarity of texture that revolutionized Wagner conducting, was a marvelous case in point, as was Heiner Müller's *Tristan und Isolde* (1993), also conducted with intense lyricism and precision by Daniel Barenboim.

Never distant from any discussion of Wagner since World War II has been the vexed question of his anti-Semitism and its relationship to his music. Wagner's prose writings, and, of course, Cosima's diaries, provide ample evidence of a powerful and relentless anti-Semitic consciousness, although, as Dieter Borchmeyer has pointed out, it was not consistently the same and not as simple as has often been suggested.[1] It went through several developments, was influenced by the French more than the Germans, and, says Borchmeyer, was quite different from Hitler's and the Nazis. I have already written about this elsewhere, so I do not want to repeat what I have said before, except to say that I do not think that Wagner's highly problematic social, political, and racial theories (which he himself changed many times in the course of his extremely prolific career) can be surgically separated from the music dramas.[2] But it is also evident that none of the operas contain explicitly anti-Semitic material—there are no Jewish characters, for instance—and that fact therefore requires extreme caution in making direct leaps from his discursive writings to characters, situations, and even musical passages in operas like *Die Meistersinger* and *Siegfried.* Ever since the appearance in 1952 of Adorno's pathbreaking book *In Search of Wagner*, an often acrimonious debate has raged over how to interpret the operas in light of the man's xenophobic and defamatory anti-Semitism.[3] At one extreme there are the excesses of Paul Lawrence Rose, who asserts that every single note of the *Ring*, for instance, is drenched in anti-Semitic hatred; to listen to Siegfried's funeral music in *Götterdämmerung* and then to the funeral march in Beethoven's *Eroica* is, Rose says implausibly, to be filled with hatred of the Jews in the first instance, and in the second ennobled and dignified.[4] This is far beyond anything that Adorno says about Wagner's depictions of Beckmesser, Mime, and Alberich. The difference between what Adorno and Rose conclude with is in Rose's book to devalue and banish Wagner's work, while Adorno has the effect of encouraging a critical demystifying freedom to look at an aesthetic achievement despite its weaknesses, which remain very considerable. But, to repeat, trying to deal with Wagner's racial ideology in enormously complex operas like *Die Meistersinger* and *Siegfried* runs the danger of misreading clues and of forcing traces of suspect attitudes into altogether too rigid a framework of ubiquitous anti-Semitism that is ultimately indebted not so much to Wagner himself, but to his later disciples Stewart Chamberlain and Hitler. There is a classic refutation of these suspect procedures by Hans Vaget, who meticulously reanalyzes the "Jew in the Brambles" Grimm's fairy tale, which was adduced first by Adorno, then with less restraint by Barry Millington, in order to say that Wagner's characterization of

Beckmesser in *Die Meistersinger* is really a viciously racist stereotype of a Jew.[5] Without summarizing the whole debate, I shall only say here that Vaget shows the limits of what can be done with such evidence by more carefully interpreting the fairy tale and then showing how, despite its intertextual presence in the opera, its impact is very circumscribed, much more so than Adorno and Millington say. Vaget's conclusion deserves quotation in full:

> It is time to acknowledge that our entire discourse on the covert anti-Semitic agenda of Wagner's operas has been primarily fueled by later political appropriations of Wagner both during the Weimar period and the Third Reich, and not by, as it ought to have been, the evidence of the works. . . . If we want to achieve that intellectual freedom vis-à-vis Wagner, of which Adorno spoke and for which he himself strove, we will have to place the Nazi appropriation of Wagner within the appropriate historical parameters. Let us not accept the *völkisch* tack on Wagner as canonical; let us not have Houston Stewart Chamberlain and his disciple Adolf Hitler, those two most devastating Wagnerians, determine in all perpetuity how we are to read *Die Meistersinger von Nürnberg*. Only when we free ourselves from this yoke will we break that Adornian spell.[6]

At the other extreme from Rose are the various writers about Wagner (like Robert Donington and Deryck Cooke) who more or less ignore the man's egregious political ideas altogether.[7] In view of the elaborate and finally genocidal consequences of appropriating and distorting some of Wagner's ideas, and also in view of aspects of his portraits of Beckmesser and Mime, simply to avoid the anti-Semitism in what can seem to be its alliance with the magical power of Wagner's theatrical and musical craft is insufficient. A provocatively intelligent approach to the question, quite new and not weighted down with prepackaged notions about Wagner that simply misunderstand the music, is pioneered by Marc Weiner in *Richard Wagner and the Anti-Semitic Imagination*.[8] A cultural historian and a Germanist, Weiner sets Wagner within an ensemble of beliefs about Jews—especially the peculiarities of the Jewish body—and proceeds from there to show how characters like Beckmesser, Kundry, Hagen, and others are created out of a set of negative attitudes about their voices, feet, smell, eyes, and overall degeneration; such characteristics as an effeminate voice, a clubfoot, a smell of pitch or sweat are countered by Wagnerian antidotes such as the Heldentenor, a heroic physique, healthiness, and so on. Weiner's intention is not to rubbish Wagner, but in a minute way to trace the archeology of recurring patterns in the works to specific aspects of an anti-Semitic iconography in which Wagner was immersed. As reviewers of Weiner's book have said, however, he does not provide the reader with evidence that audiences during Wagner's own time, or thereafter during the Weimar and Nazi periods, registered any recognition of this or indicated that they had deciphered the signs.[9] Illuminating though they may be, therefore, Weiner's brilliant and informative speculations lack sufficient empirical proof that what he finds in Wagner was in fact put there by him and seen there by his contemporaries.

Very few of the commentators who depend on Adorno's *In Search of Wagner* for their critique of Wagner's various shortcomings seem to be aware of a late return to the composer in a remarkable lecture given by Adorno in 1963 and published one year later in the Bayreuth Festival program.[10] Many of his earlier strictures against Wagner were tempered, if not altogether withdrawn in the lecture, but what he ventures for the first time is, I believe, very useful in trying to approach a work like *Die Meistersinger von Nürnberg* now. (It should be noted, however, that Adorno is still very harsh about Wagner's anti-Semitism.) As Pierre Boulez was also to say, Adorno confesses that his "own experience with Wagner does not exhaust itself in the political content, as unredeemable as the latter is, and I often have the impression that in laying it bare I have cleared away one level only to see another emerge from underneath."[11] Underlining his sense that he now gives the aesthetic a new priority in examining Wagner's oeuvre, Adorno adds:

> But what has changed about Wagner, in the interim, is not merely his impact on others, but his work itself, in itself. This is what forms his relevance [for today]; not some posthumous second triumph or the well-justified defeat of the neo-Baroque [e.g., Stravinsky's neoclassicism]. As spiritual entities, works of art are not complete in themselves. They create a magnetic field of all possible intentions and forces, of inner tendencies and countervailing ones, of successful and necessarily unsuccessful elements. Objectively, new layers are constantly detaching themselves, emerging from within; others grow irrelevant and die off. One relates to a work of

> art not merely, as is often said, by adapting it to fit a new situation, but rather by deciphering *within* it things to which one has a historically different reaction.[12]

What now appears to Adorno as among the most important of Wagner's achievements and characteristics is his musical nominalism—that is, his capacity for going against the general character of operas as he inherited them in order to press his case for the irreducibly particular:

> He was the first to draw the consequences from the contradiction between traditional forms, indeed the traditional formal language of music as a whole, and the concrete artistic tasks at hand. . . . He clearly faced the contradiction between the general and the particular in music, which until then had been crystallizing in mere unconsciousness, and his *ingenium* made its incorruptible decision that nothing general should exist, except in the extreme of particularity.[13]

This decision involved Wagner in the forging of an infinitely plastic and detailed style that was responsive to each particular action, situation, and changing character in his work, hence endless melody, the elimination of "numbers," and the invention of leitmotifs, which run an extraordinary gamut of rhythmic, harmonic, aural, and coloristic elements, that show his amazing gifts as a technician of sound in which an almost miraculous capacity for constant change—"irregularity" Adorno calls it—assures that the music is always interesting, never routine. Thus, Adorno adds that, in *Die Meistersinger*, Wagner dispensed with the chromaticism of *Tristan* and was still able to achieve "a concreteness of the irregular that traditional music never dreamed of. This would remain prototypical for Schoenberg, for Berg, and for the most recent tendency: the trend towards structures that are free, yet dense."[14] An example of this irregularity occurs near the beginning of *Die Meistersinger*, just after the overture ends as the orchestra is going through its cadential flourishes in subdominant-tonic sequence; then, as the curtain rises, it suddenly flows directly into a four-part Lutheran chorale sung by chorus and organ. Wagner interrupts this regular flow with orchestral interventions in a totally different vein, which he uses to accompany a silent languishing (*schmachtende*) interchange between Walther von Stolzing and Eva.

Adorno is especially right to note that for this irregular style we have to see in Wagner the radicalized "artistic consciousness of an antagonistic, internally contradictory world." This is the opposite of Hegel's view that, in order to produce coherent drama, we must realize that "mere desire, the wildness and brutality of the will, has no place in the theater."[15] Many of the interpretive schemes—including Wagner's own in some instances—that have been used to unlock the supposedly secret meanings of his works assume the existence of a synthetically reconciling principle that turns the works into internally consistent wholes, their parts and jagged edges finally settling down into redemptive arrangements from which all conflict has been excluded. With the possible exception of *Parsifal*, this is simply not true of Wagner's major works. Too much in them remains unsettled and refractory, like Hagen or Alberich, and when it comes to figures such as Wotan or Siegfried, or even Hans

Sachs and his concern with *Wahn*, we are taken with their wildness or brutality of will, which resist herding into some palliative or acceptable ethical structure. We find ourselves looking instead to the nominalist musical forms that Wagner uses; Adorno says that we should try to describe how, "without borrowing," his forms "express, develop, and create themselves with compelling necessity from within."[16]

Die Meistersinger, which Wagner wrote between 1861 and 1867, has a remarkably central place within Wagner's oeuvre. Already a famous—not to say notorious—figure in Europe, he was known as the composer of such important, if not fully successful works as *Lohengrin* and *Tannhäuser* (whose 1861 Paris premiere caused a legendary furor) and was handsomely embarked on the composition of his gigantic tetralogy. But he had stopped work on the *Ring* after completing act 2 of *Siegfried* in 1857 and was not to return in earnest to the work's final act until 1869. In the meantime, under the influence of a complex but finally unsatisfying relationship with Mathilde Wesendonck, he had written *Tristan und Isolde*, which he completed in 1859. Thus the great Nuremberg opera sits between *Tristan* and act 3 of *Siegfried*, both of which in harmonic idiom are far more chromatic than *Die Meistersinger*; in *Tristan*'s case the comparison is astonishing, since in that work he reaches virtually the limits of tonality, while in the Nuremberg work he has returned solidly to a diatonicism deliberately reminiscent of Bach. Everything about *Tristan*'s harmonic undecidability, its flirtation with atonality, its avoidance and deferral of tonal closure, has been all but banished from the score of *Die Meistersinger*, whose opening C major measures announce a robust, open-air relative simplicity of harmony and rhythmic pulse that radiate healthiness, vitality, affirmation. It is, in short, everything that *Tristan*, in its claustrophobic hothouse celebration of death through love, is not.

Wagner's earliest completed operas were heavily influenced by Giacomo Meyerbeer and prevailing styles of the 1830s, mostly French. After that early stage there is a reversion to Germanic themes of Wagner's own devising; he never deviated from this until the end of his career. This is also the period during which in a supremely autodidactic way he studied and digested works, both learned and creative, in which he took a great interest as part of the romantic revival of attention to mythology, philology, and folk history; in Wagner's case, his cultural readings also included a prolonged study of Greek tragedy. More than any other composer, I think, Wagner not only studied the works of others but also produced a vast output of pamphlets (including his defamatory work "Judaism in Music" and the important explorations of *Opera and Drama* in 1852), declarations, commentaries, journalistic articles, to say nothing of prose sketches of his planned music dramas, plus detailed explanations of them, that were designed to create a receptive constituency for the revolution he was trying to make. An early anarchist and friend of Mikhail Bakunin, he soon fell under the spell of Arthur Schopenhauer, whose pessimism, alleviated by faith in a redemptive art, wove its way into Wagner's mature operas, including *Die Meistersinger*, which is also the most historical of his great works. I should also mention that, while working on the opera in 1864, he began his relationship with Cosima von Bülow, Liszt's daughter and Hans von Bülow's wife. This was the most lasting and fulfilling attachment to a woman (and a formidable one at that) that he ever formed; they remained together until his death in 1883.

There are fascinating parallels between Berlioz and Wagner, but profound divergences, too. Both were autodidacts and highly original musical and dramatic innovators who were well known as musicians and eccentrics. Yet Berlioz was, I think, principally concerned with the techniques, rather than the philosophy, of music and drama, while Wagner was not just a reformer and active revolutionary, but a theoretician and philosopher as well. Both men saw themselves as linked spiritually to Beethoven, whose *Fidelio* they were especially impressed with as much for its power and vitality as for its portrayal of a woman whose love and constancy in Wagner's case would win out over the destruction of the whole world (Brünnhilde at the end of the *Ring*); Berlioz's Dido is a more tragic and flawed figure, although she, too, is symbolic of a feminine capacity for oversize emotions. But it is as composers of opera that attempt to represent history that Wagner and Berlioz are instructively different from each other. *Les Troyens* is based mainly on a great literary passion, not on philological or archeological research. The specific details about costume, gesture, character, and instrumentation on which Berlioz lavished much attention derived from impressions and miscellaneous reading and looking at art rather than on sustained and systematic inquiry into the Roman world for which, to the composer, Virgil's great imperial epic was a sufficient basis for nineteenth-century representation.

Wagner was altogether more methodical in his approach to the historical subject matter—Hans Sachs and sixteenth-century Nuremberg—than that. He began thinking about the opera as early as 1845, and intermittently during the years leading up to the first draft of the libretto he read copiously, if not always systematically, on the history of the town and its time. For this he consulted Grimm's compilations and Wagenseil's *Nuremberg Chronicle* (1697), and according to John Warrack he also drew on contemporary writers such as E. T. A. Hoffmann, Friedrich Furchau, and August Hagen, in addition to the work of composers such as Albert Lortzing.[17] If, for Berlioz, Aeneas's mission to establish an empire in Italy is portrayed allusively as having application to the current French empire under Louis-Napoléon, Wagner's Nuremberg was even more pointedly constructed as an idealized picture of sixteenth-century Germany with specific reference to the problems of Germany during the 1850s and 1860s. Of these problems, the matter of German identity and its particularly urgent aesthetic mission, in which Wagner obviously sees himself playing a central role through the character of Hans Sachs, are the most important. For this specific purpose, Wagner uses *Die Meistersinger* as an opera deliberately *not* set in the mythological or legendary realm (as had been the case with the *Ring* and *Tristan*), since what he now seemed anxious to tackle was the very act of artistic creation, a creation set in a concrete, historically material world with a direct bearing on his own.

"Most operatic characters," according to Edward Cone in his seminal essay "The World of Opera and Its Inhabitants," "are musicians who compose songs or sing songs composed by their friends!"[18] The subject of *Die Meistersinger* is in fact the composition or creation of a song, and its main characters are singers, with the difference in Wagner that they are also portrayed as craftsmen and proud citizens; the three attributes flow together in all cases except that of the young hero, Walther von Stolzing. He is an outsider and a nobleman who, because of his love for Eva, Veit Pogner's daughter, wants to join the brotherhood of Meistersingers and can only do so by undergoing a trial. Quite a number of Wagner's major works, especially after *Tristan*, contain within them a brotherhood of like-minded companions, as if it was necessary for his imagination to see individuals as belonging to a group bound together by occupation and avocation as in *Die Meistersinger*, by religion and cause as in *Parsifal*, or by blood as in the clans and tribes that people the *Ring*. Nuremberg's distinction in this roster is that it was chosen by Wagner because of its centrality to the history of Germany, its people forming an idealized portrait of what he took to be the quintessential German community disclosing itself through the opera's action. At its center stands the guild of Meistersingers whose avocation—the composition and performance of songs according to strict rules—represents for Wagner the prototypical German function, emblematic of work, tradition, national identity, and individual genius. Serenus Zeitblom, Thomas Mann's narrator in *Doktor Faustus* (1947), his postwar novel about the great German composer, suggests much the same thing: as Adrian Leverkühn's fortunes and achievements and sins go, so also goes Germany. Thus, in *Die Meistersinger*, the crux of the opera is whether Walther von Stolzing, a German from another community, can be admitted into a fraternity that has ringed itself with rituals and tests making membership difficult, but potentially open to a combination of creative innovation and tradition-observing art, of which in a sense neither they nor Walther have a preconceived idea. There is no formula, since it is clear from the first act that pure naive artistry will not do, whereas someone like Beckmesser or Kothner who knows all the rules cannot himself do more than remanipulate them, albeit without ingenuity or freshness. This is why Hans Sachs hovers near the creative and traditional center of the town and the fraternity; like Walther, he is capable of understanding art as creation, and like Walther, too, he is attracted to Eva. Because of his age and Schopenhauerian disillusionment, however, Sachs withdraws from both the artistic and amorous competition in order to direct and channel the younger generation together. In act 3, he tells Eva that he has no wish to be a King Marke, the character in *Tristan* whose wife Isolde illicitly loves Tristan.

Thus *Die Meistersinger*, which takes place over the evening before and the day of Midsummer, enacts the search for a middle way at a moment of dangerous extremes and impossible situations, which Wagner represents in various ways throughout the opera. There is in the first act Walther's fury at the Meistersingers' pedantry, which, in his opinion, unfairly disqualifies him from membership after he sings his first trial song. Then there is Beckmesser's extreme jealousy and his hypertrophied sense of musical tradition, which turn him into Walther's implacable enemy. Moreover, both men are carefully watched by a whole group of young apprentices led by David, Sachs's assistant, who represent the new generation of aspirants for whom the difficulties of getting into the Meistersingers' group reflect what they must soon go through. Then, too, there are the senior men like Pogner, Kothner, Sachs, and the others who as a middle-class burgher elite represent the town's interests, as well as a consciousness of somehow bearing responsibility for the fate of the German burgher who alone in Germany cares about, nurtures, and promotes art. As Veit Pogner, Eva's father, puts it in act 1 when he addresses the assembled guild, burghers care about art, and hence also about the good and the true. To this end he announces that, since the next day is the Midsummer festival and traditional song contest of St. John's Day (Johannistag), he wants to show his seriousness about the group's mission by offering his only daughter as the prize for the winner. Though this may seem like making a woman into little more than a chattel, Pogner also says that she would have the final choice of husband, though she must marry a Meistersinger.

All of these events together constitute an interrelated series of impasses, blockages, impediments that have the power and in some cases actually do threaten not only Nuremberg's present state but also—and much more important—its future. At the center of attention is the question of Eva's marriage, the continuity of generations that Wagner braids together with the ability to pass a singing test, win the contest, and the bride. The opera highlights and dramatizes the obstacles by identifying the ability to create with the possibility of procreation; both are continuities assuring Nuremberg's and Germany's coherent identity and its potential for extension into the future. Acts 1 and 2 lay forth the problems and, with consummate skill, show Sachs as the one person within all communities who can mediate between the contestants. He is an enabler, as when he persuades the thoroughly disgusted and angry Walther that he should enter the contest, but he is also capable of stopping actions that may threaten continuity and consequently the whole town. In short, Sachs, along with Eva and Walther, inhabits the potentially creative middle, even though Sachs rules himself out as a contender for Eva's hand, despite her obvious interest in him. One of the most intriguing things about the opera is this unmistakable amorous triangulation at the center: Sachs and Eva vacillate between coy approaches and withdrawals, Sachs obviously plays a paternal role with Walther, and so forth.

The middle act of this extraordinarily charted and patterned opera contains two actions undertaken by Sachs whose purpose is to prevent a complete breakdown of the ongoing action. One is to persuade Eva and Walther not to elope. The other is to stymie Beckmesser's efforts to serenade Eva, since it is clear from act 1 that Beckmesser is a most unlikely suitor and in act 2 it is horrendously evident from the dreadful—but musically advanced—ditty he sings to Pogner's daughter from the street. Sachs determinedly overpowers the Marker's singing with his tapping and his singing; the climactic scene is a musical montage of one man singing against the bangings of the other. It bears noting that here, as well as during acts 1 and 3, a small set of frequently repeated biblical allusions reinforce Wagner's contemporary concerns. Hans in German is a short form of Johannes: Sachs as the preparer and announcer, the avatar of something or someone that will come after him and complete the process of rebirth that is in fact symbolized by John's function as the Baptist. In the opening scene of act 3, David presents himself to Sachs and announces that he wishes to marry Magdalena, Eva's companion; he also announces that he has written a song for Johannistag, for which Wagner uses the tune of the opera's opening chorale. What David does in the ditty is to describe the voyage of a German woman to the Jordan River looking for John the Baptist, only to discover that the Jordan has in fact become the River Teplitz, which runs through Nuremberg, where John has become Hans, David's master. Similarly, Sachs's raucous ballad in act 2 that so disturbs Beckmesser is about Eva leaving Paradise and requiring shoes for her bare feet—hence the need for a shoemaker, the very profession that Sachs has pursued. These, and several other references to both the Old and New Testaments, have the effect of typologically knotting together religious and secular time, providing what takes place in Nuremberg with a figural density that Wagner will return to in *Parsifal*.[19]

Wagner's extended musical and dramatic image for what lies in store for the city if extremes get the upper hand is the disquieting riot that closes act 2. What makes this scene so disconcerting is that David's beating of the hapless Beckmesser is what starts it off and in which the young apprentice takes some pride the next day. Wagner intends the scene to symbolize the total chaos that ensues once restraint and poor art are not controlled, but unfortunately this scene, plus the contest in act 3, also form a sadistic punishment for the hopelessly out-of-control Beckmesser, in whose fury and pain Sachs and his robust fellow townsmen take an unsettling pleasure. It is difficult not to connect this savage scapegoating of one admittedly peculiar citizen with the salutary achievements of German art and society that Sachs says in his final peroration must be vigorously defended. The punishment and banishment of an unacceptable outsider (Walther von Stolzing is an outsider, too, but since he is noble, young, and blond—and played that way in traditional stagings—he is acceptable) seems to be required if Nuremberg is to proceed to fulfill its exemplary, even prophetic destiny. Marc Weiner perceptively shows how pitch (*Pech* in German), which Sachs uses in his cobbling trade, is often referred to in the work whenever Beckmesser is about; and Weiner is probably also right when he shows that pitch's color and unpleasant smell might in Wagner be associated with a Jew's stench.[20] He proceeds to suggest that the nasty smell of pitch is countered by a whole set of pleasant associations that Wagner makes with the elder or lilac trees (the German word *Flieder* could refer to either) whose aroma "has its roots in diverse cultural traditions of Wagner's homeland." Thus: "After he has been soundly battered and ridiculed, the audacity of the Jew's intrusion into the social-aesthetic and sexual sphere of purist musical Germany is made manifest. With the magical aromatic breeze the elder tree has rid Germany of its presumptuous foe, and Nuremberg's evil spirit, the devilish Beckmesser, has been exorcised."[21]

As I said earlier, the only difficulty with this perspective is that it fixes matters too much. It is also possible to associate what Wagner is doing with common scapegoating techniques in most societies, as well as with a quite prevalent mid-nineteenth-century cultural need to produce, portray, and represent a paradigmatic community at a moment in history that is felt to be extremely fractious because it is on the verge of great change. Besides, Wagner never suggests that until he is driven crazy by lust and jealousy Beckmesser is non-German, or has not been a worthy Meistersinger, or has always been an incompetent sneak. Even if we accept the supposition that Wagner's most likely immediate target is Beckmesser as undesirable misfit, it is also the case that Wagner's purpose in *Die Meistersinger* is not only to viciously cast out an unharmonious person from the polity, but also to do something quite different as well; I see the two possibilities as compatible with each other, and that, I also think, adds to the opera's aesthetic complexities as well as to its problematic, if not downright troubling, character. The burden of the first part of act 3 is not only to snare Beckmesser into stealing a manuscript from Sachs's table, but also to present Sachs's view of the world in his celebrated monologue "Wahn! Wahn! Überall Wahn!" and to let him guide Walther from exasperation and dream into the composition of a superb new song. This becomes the penultimate version of the Preislied, which Walther will repeat in an altered and shortened form in order to win the contest.

Once again, the question of aesthetic creativity is associated not simply with gaining a bride, but essentially with Sachs's vision that musical genius must take an acceptable social form in order for it to give life to the community—in order for it to breathe spirit and animate coherence into what might otherwise degenerate into social incoherence and the kind of chaos we saw during the final moments of act 2. At the end of Walther's recitation of his dream, therefore, after commenting technically on each of the strophes, Sachs compliments the young man on his achievement and then baptizes the song as he might a child.

Sachs christens the song with a rather ponderous name—"die selige Morgentraum-Deutweise"—whose godparents, as he calls them, are the assembled little group of listeners. In the great G flat major polyphonic quintet that follows, they each use the song's meaning and imagery to subdue by reflection and interpretation whatever in their hearts threatens the orderly natural progression portended by the song, from morning to evening, from baptism to birth, from idealized to consummated love.

Wagner's goal in *Die Meistersinger* gains in substance and interest if we look briefly at a near-contemporary prose work, George Eliot's *Middlemarch* (1872), which places a similar emphasis on the relationship between social coherence and an aesthetic medium. To understand why Wagner assigned so strenuous a significance to music, we will be helped by remembering that in the "Prelude" to her novel, Eliot diagnoses the problem of contemporary individuals motivated by a sense of vocation and pilgrimage; individuals who, like Saint Theresa, require an epic life for it, "wherein there was a constant unfolding of far-resonant action." In this age, Eliot goes on to explain, "these later-born Theresas were helped by no coherent social faith and order which could perform the function of knowledge for the ardently willing soul."[22] To rectify this lack, therefore, the novelist will attempt to create a hospitable structure and medium for an otherwise anonymous Saint Theresa, which will in turn be nothing less than a sort of group portrait of Middlemarch, a middling English town from whose vantage point one can discern the outlines of the entire English polity. This striking parallel with Wagner's conception of Nuremberg as being the center of Germany is complemented by Eliot's identification of Middlemarch's common life—"the same embroiled medium, the same troublous fitfully-illuminated life"—with language, or at least the kind of dynamically coherent perspective on the change, variety, ups and downs of life that language can offer.[23] In the following passage from the novel, note the interweaving of rhetorical and literary images that not only indicates a very high degree of self-consciousness about the constructive act of producing (reproducing) a life, but also associates the coherence of perspective with a coherent rendering of social life. I take this passage to be normative in much the same way that Wagner calculated the effect of *Die Meistersinger* for the modern German situation:

> But any one watching keenly the stealthy convergence of human lots, sees a slow preparation of effects from one life on another, which tells like a calculated irony on the indifference or the frozen stare with which we look at our unintroduced neighbour. Destiny stands by sarcastic with our *dramatis personae* folded in her hand.
>
> Old provincial society had its share of this subtle movement: had not only its striking downfalls . . . but also those less marked vicissitudes which are constantly shifting the boundaries of social intercourse, and begetting new consciousness of interdependence.[24]

Eliot then talks about those "families that stood with rocky firmness amid all this fluctuation, [who] were slowly presenting new aspects in spite of solidity, and altering with the double change of self and beholder."[25] In both novel and opera, social movement is regulated by the rhythms and resonances of a medium that unfolds in all sorts of ways, but that seem to imitate, and perhaps even replicate, the movement of natural generation: a song is born by collaboration in Wagner, a new consciousness of interdependence is "begotten" in Eliot. These fertilizations of society associate social coherence and creativity with each other, since, as Eliot says, without something like that there can be no integrated social faith and order. For Wagner, the project is threatened by what in the magnificent monologue that opens act 3, the morning after the riotous turbulence of the preceding evening, he calls "Wahn," a difficult word to translate since it combines illusion and madness. The brilliance of the monologue is that Sachs is able to stand outside the action by virtue of his age and gifts of wisdom and sympathy; he can discern the gnawing restlessness of Wahn as it insinuates itself in society, since there is no escaping its machinations, and he also resolves to put it to fructifying use through Walther's passion for Eva and song. In the passage that concludes the opera, Sachs not only speaks with the authority of Nuremberg's sage, but also with Wagner's; this is as close as we come to the composer's point of view.

Sachs in effect is both a Dionysian and an Apollonian personage, and perhaps more of the latter than the former. Wagner and Cosima met Friedrich Nietzsche just as *Die Meistersinger* was being completed, and one could suggest that the passages on Euripides in *The Birth of Tragedy* (1872) owe something to the figure of Sachs, who, although he plays the role of Walther's mentor, is also a coauthor of the Meisterlied that wins the day and climaxes Nuremberg's apotheosis at the end of the opera.[26] What Walther sings at the contest is the third version of his creation, which enables him to combine the absolute purity of prelapsarian Paradise (we recall that Eva is associated with Eve in act 2) with the fertilizing creative energy of Parnassus.

Two somewhat related points in conclusion. Both in its music and setting *Die Meistersinger* provides a conscious alternative to the doom-ridden, ominously circular world of the *Ring* and *Tristan*, two works that surround his only realistic and comic opera. Even if Sachs believes that in the end everything is Wahn, the solid, down-to-earth four-squareness of Nuremberg is there to furnish at least a temporary option to counteract the mystifying pessimism of what he would return to in *Siegfried* and *Götterdämmerung*. Compositionally *Meistersinger* has none of the interwoven retrospective narratives by which the *Ring*'s major characters—Wotan most especially—try futilely to retell their own stories in desperate hope that by going back far enough yet one more time they might find respite from the circular doom that Adorno thought was one of Wagner's great weaknesses.[27] Wagner's way of sidestepping this quandary in his centralizing Nuremberg opera was to return to the classical archaizing idiom of Johann Sebastian Bach, whose contrapuntal skill is memorialized and rivaled in part by Wagner himself. Cosima's diaries are full of Richard's comments about Bach as a self-sufficient cosmic system with its own sun, stars, and satellites, of Bach as a great tree casting its shade over all music, Bach as the source of everything, and so on.[28] For Wagner's generation (and, as Charles Rosen well describes it, for Chopin,

Schumann, and Liszt) Bach represents not just a primary source for music, but he induces in his admirers a passion for contrapuntal style;[29] hence in *Die Meistersinger* the skillful polyphonic lines, which—though they have been unjustly disparaged by Adorno, among others, as not real counterpoint but only a clever way of combining themes—have the effect of producing an archaizing classicism that echoes that of the earlier German master.[30] The paradox is, however, that an opera set in the mid-sixteenth century should use a late seventeenth-century idiom while simultaneously proclaiming the diatonic naturalness and health that Wagner had eschewed completely in the *Ring* and *Tristan*. Carl Dahlhaus reminds us that "Wagner's fundamental aesthetic conviction, which he shared with Kant, was that art, in order to be art, must conceal itself and appear in the guise of nature."[31] We can respond sympathetically to Sachs and Walther because what they sing has the familiarity of a kind of historicized lyricism, supported by an orchestral texture that is simultaneously as accessible, as contrapuntally learned, and as ingeniously transformative as anything Wagner ever wrote. The devious, choleric, unattractive Beckmesser by comparison sings dissonantly and unpleasingly, although his musical idiom is harmonically more advanced than that of any other character.

Dahlhaus also observes that Wagner's music in this opera has the quality of a reminiscence, distant and yet directly appealing because of its diatonic harmonies, which repress chromaticism.[32] This is one reason why Beckmesser, the *diabolus in musica*, and the guild of Meistersingers are in the opera, the former expelled, the latter to incorporate Walther. But it is also why Sachs must have the last word and associate this middle-class microcosm of Germany with the preservation and care of German art, which they have kept "Deutsch und wahr" (German and true) even after the aristocracy has abandoned its responsibility. His warnings against the threat of foreign rule are not likely to endear him to proponents of hybridity and multiculturalism. Yet what he warns about is the extremely commonplace fear of the loss of authentic tradition; to today's audience this presents no particularly unfamiliar aspect of public discourse since it seems to be there in every kind of nationalist and/or identity politics. To ascribe to it something uniquely German, and therefore protofascist, is insidious to say the least, since no nationalism that I know of can escape criticism on that score. The question is whether the opera is parochially only about German art and tradition or whether to non-German audiences it makes more universal sense than that. I certainly think so, but I think also that its message of a proclaimed national integrity is vulnerable to the kind of distortions for which the infamous Nuremberg racial laws and the Nazi era itself provide the most damning evidence. Yet in Sachs's pleas for art and a flexible understanding of its rules we are well-placed today to discern a countertruth coexisting with the putative xenophobia that Sachs seems to be upholding. For the modern interpreter it suffices to see the two possibilities, and then to emphasize the more humane one over the other without obliterating what still unsettles and disturbs us about this complex, bristling work of genius.

NOTES

INTRODUCTION

1. Te-hsing Shan, "An Interview with Edward W. Said," in *Interviews with Edward W. Said*, ed. Amritjit Singh and Bruce Johnson (Jackson: University Press of Mississippi, 2004), 125.
2. Te-hsing Shan, "Power, Politics, and Culture: An Interview with Edward W. Said," *Tamkang Review* 44, no. 1 (2013): 155.
3. Outline for "Authority and Transgression in Opera," October 23, 1996, box 33, folder 8, Edward W. Said Papers, Columbia University Library.
4. Edward Said, "Music and Feminism," *Nation*, February 7, 1987, 158–60. When first being introduced to McClary's work in the late 1980s, he thought that it was "good stuff"; Edward Said to Greg Sandow, March 2, 1987, box 155, folder 21, Edward W. Said Papers.
5. Edward Said, "The Imperial Spectacle," *Grand Street* 6, no. 2 (1987): 82–104; revised and republished in *Culture and Imperialism* (London: Chatto and Windus, 1993), 133–59.
6. Said, *Culture and Imperialism*, 59–60.
7. This *Fidelio* production, directed by Alexander Schulin and conducted by Barenboim, was performed by the Chicago Symphony Orchestra in May 1998. Said's narration is preserved in box 109, folder 13, of the Edward W. Said Papers.

8. Edward Said to Gerard Mortier, June 25, 1998, box 28, folder 14; Gerard Mortier to Edward Said, July 17, 1998, box 23, folder 5, Edward W. Said Papers.
9. Edward Said to the chair of the faculty of English at Cambridge University, December 11, 1995, box 33, folder 8, Edward W. Said Papers.
10. Chair of the faculty of English at Cambridge University to Edward Said, January 2, 1996, box 33, folder 8, Edward W. Said Papers; senior commissioning editor at Cambridge University Press to Edward Said, January 25, 1996, box 33, folder 8, Edward W. Said Papers.
11. Edward Said, *Musical Elaborations* (New York: Columbia University Press, 1991), xvii, xxi.
12. Most of these essays were republished in Edward Said, *Music at the Limits* (New York: Columbia University Press, 2008). Some of Said's work on opera is also included in Daniel Barenboim and Edward Said, *Parallels and Paradoxes: Explorations in Music and Society*, ed. Ara Guzelimian (New York: Pantheon, 2002); and Edward Said, *On Late Style: Music and Literature Against the Grain* (New York: Pantheon, 2006). Two of his contributions on opera in *Grand Street* have not been republished in books: a short piece on Olivier Messiaen's *Saint François d'Assise* (1983) in *Grand Street*, no. 36 (1990): 119–21; and a public conversation with Peter Sellars in *Grand Street*, no. 61 (1997): 193–207.
13. Several letters by editors and board members of musicological journals are preserved in the Edward W. Said Papers—for instance, Arthur Groos to Edward Said, October 9, 1987, box 10, folder 11; Jeffrey Kallberg to Edward Said, March 3, 1993, box 36, folder 36; Michael Long to Edward Said, January 11, 1996, box 21, folder 11; and Ralph Locke to Edward Said, March 12, 1998, box 94, folder 2.
14. The Edward W. Said Papers preserve correspondence with many music scholars, including Anthony Barone, Leon Botstein, Edward Cone, John Deathridge, Jane Fulcher, Christopher Gibbs, Ralph Locke, Susan McClary, Donald Mitchell, Jean-Jacques Nattiez, Ali Jihad Racy, Maynard Solomon, and Rose Rosengard Subotnik, to name a few. Said tried to publish books by several of these scholars in his Harvard book series, Convergences: Inventories of the Present, and he successfully published Jeffrey Kallberg's *Chopin at the Boundaries: Sex, History, and Musical Genre* (Cambridge, Mass.: Harvard University Press, 1996); and Linda and Michael Hutcheon's *Opera: The Art of Dying* (Cambridge, Mass.: Harvard University Press, 2004).

15. Said, *Musical Elaborations*, xxi.
16. Course materials for Opera and Society, spring 1995, box 95, folder 14, Edward W. Said Papers.
17. Course notebook for Opera and Society, spring 1995, box 95, folder 14, Edward W. Said Papers.
18. Edward Said, "*Così fan tutte* at the Limits," *Grand Street*, no. 62 (1997): 93–106; "On *Fidelio*," *London Review of Books*, October 30, 1997, 25–28.

1. *COSÌ FAN TUTTE* AT THE LIMITS

1. Charles Rosen, *The Classical Style: Haydn, Mozart, Beethoven* (New York: Viking, 1971), 314.
2. Rosen, *Classical Style*, 315.
3. Ignaz Ritter von Seyfried, "Anhang," in *Ludwig van Beethoven Studien* (Vienna: Haslinger, 1832), 22; Ludwig Rellstab, *Aus meinem Leben* (Berlin: J. Guttentag, 1861), 2:240; Franz Wegeler, *Beethoven Remembered: The Biographical Notes of Franz Wegeler and Fedinand Ries* (Arlington, Va.: Great Ocean, 1987), 153.
4. Emily Anderson, ed., *The Letters of Beethoven* (London: Macmillan, 1961), 1:334; Oscar George Sonneck, ed., *Beethoven: Impressions of Contemporaries* (New York: G. Schirmer, 1926), 22.
5. Rosen, *Classical Style*, 314–17; Scott Burnham, "Mozart's felix culpa: *Così fan tutte* and the Irony of Beauty," *Musical Quarterly* 78, no. 1 (1994): 77–98.
6. R. P. Blackmur, *The Lion and the Honeycomb: Essays in Solicitude and Critique* (New York: Harcourt, Brace, 1955), 199.
7. Alan Tyson, "Notes on the Composition of Mozart's *Così fan tutte*," *Journal of the American Musicological Society* 37, no. 2 (1984): 356–401.
8. Theodor W. Adorno, "On the Fetish-Character in Music and the Regression of Listening," in *The Essential Frankfurt School Reader*, ed. Andrew Arato and Eike Gebhardt (New York: Urizen, 1978), 270–99.
9. Andrew Steptoe, *The Mozart–Da Ponte Operas: The Cultural and Musical Background to Le nozze di Figaro, Don Giovanni, and Così fan tutte* (Oxford: Clarendon, 1988), 208–42.
10. Steptoe, *Mozart–Da Ponte Operas*, 208–9.
11. Steptoe, 209.
12. Mozart quoted in Steptoe, 87–88.

13. Steptoe, 90.
14. Mozart quoted in Steptoe, 90.
15. Steptoe, 213.
16. Michel Foucault, *The Order of Things: An Archaeology of the Human Sciences* (New York: Pantheon, 1970), 209–10. The addition between square brackets is Said's.
17. Foucault, *Order of Things*, 209.
18. Foucault, 211.
19. Maynard Solomon, *Mozart: A Life* (New York: HarperCollins, 1995).
20. Emily Anderson, ed., *The Letters of Mozart and His Family* (London: Macmillan, 1966), 3:1351.
21. Donald Mitchell, *Cradles of the New: Writings on Music, 1951–1991* (London: Faber and Faber, 1995), 132. The additions between square brackets are Said's.

2. *FIDELIO*'S DIFFICULTIES WITH THE PAST

1. I have not been able to trace this text by John Eliot Gardiner. Said cites from the program booklet of a *Leonore* performance by Gardiner and the Orchestre Révolutionnaire et Romantique in New York's Avery Fisher Hall in August 1996.
2. Maynard Solomon, *Beethoven* (New York: Schirmer, 1977), 223, 222.
3. Solomon, *Beethoven*, 223.
4. Scott Burnham, *Beethoven Hero* (Princeton, N.J.: Princeton University Press, 1995); Paul Robinson, "*Fidelio* and the French Revolution," *Cambridge Opera Journal* 3, no. 1 (1991): 23–48.
5. Emily Anderson, ed., *The Letters of Beethoven* (London: Macmillan, 1961), 1:134.
6. Carl Dahlhaus, *Ludwig van Beethoven: Approaches to His Music*, trans. Mary Whittall (Oxford: Clarendon, 1991), 181–88.
7. Theodor W. Adorno, "Bourgeois Opera," in *Opera Through Other Eyes*, ed. David J. Levin (Stanford, Calif.: Stanford University Press, 1993), 34.
8. Dahlhaus, *Ludwig van Beethoven*, 185–88.
9. Rose Rosengard Subotnik, *Developing Variations: Style and Ideology in Western Music* (Minneapolis: University of Minnesota Press, 1991), 20–21. The additions between square brackets are Said's.

10. Herbert Lindenberger, *Opera: The Extravagant Art* (Ithaca, N.Y.: Cornell University Press, 1984), 15.
11. Solomon, *Beethoven*, 198–200.
12. Maynard Solomon, "Beethoven, Sonata, and Utopia," *Telos*, no. 9 (1971): 34–35. The addition between square brackets is Said's.
13. Solomon, "Beethoven, Sonata, and Utopia," 38, 40, 42.
14. Alban Berg, "A Lecture on *Wozzeck*," in *Alban Berg: Wozzeck*, ed. Douglas Jarman (Cambridge: Cambridge University Press, 1989), 154.
15. Solomon, "Beethoven, Sonata, and Utopia," 43–44.
16. M. H. Abrams, *Natural Supernaturalism: Tradition and Revolution in Romantic Literature* (New York: Norton, 1971), 64, 65.
17. Theodor Adorno, "Late Style in Beethoven," *Raritan* 13, no. 1 (1993): 106.
18. Adorno, "Late Style in Beethoven," 107.

3. *LES TROYENS* AND THE OBLIGATION TO EMPIRE

1. Jacques Barzun, *Berlioz and the Romantic Century*, 2 vols. (Boston: Little, Brown, 1950).
2. The first complete performance of *Les Troyens* in Paris was staged in 2003, conducted by John Eliot Gardiner at the Théâtre du Châtelet. Previous stagings in Paris were cut to different degrees; for instance, the production that opened the Opéra Bastille in 1990, with which Said was probably familiar, was performed without the ballets.
3. Hector Berlioz, *Beethoven by Berlioz*, trans. Ralph de Sola (Boston: Crescendo, 1975), 50.
4. Charles Rosen, *The Romantic Generation* (Cambridge, Mass.: Harvard University Press, 1995), 543.
5. Mendelssohn quoted in Rosen, *Romantic Generation*, 542.
6. Pierre Boulez, *Orientations: Collected Writings*, ed. Jean-Jacques Nattiez (Cambridge, Mass.: Harvard University Press, 1986), 212.
7. Boulez, *Orientations*, 213.
8. Jane Fulcher, *The Nation's Image: French Grand Opera as Politics and Politicized Art* (Cambridge: Cambridge University Press, 1987).
9. Fulcher, *Nation's Image*, 94–100.
10. Fulcher, 95.
11. Julian Rushton, "The Overture to *Les Troyens*," *Music Analysis* 4, nos. 1–2 (1985): 119–44; Hugh MacDonald, "*Les Troyens* at the Théâtre-Lyrique,"

3. *LES TROYENS* AND THE OBLIGATION TO EMPIRE

Musical Times 110 (1969): 919–21; D. Kern Holoman, *Berlioz* (Cambridge, Mass.: Harvard University Press, 1989), 498–540.

12. Julien Tiersot, "Lettres de Berlioz sur *Les Troyens*," *La Revue de Paris* 4 (1921): 468.
13. Jacques Barzun, *Berlioz and His Century: An Introduction to the Age of Romanticism* (Chicago: University of Chicago Press, 1982), 191–92.
14. Barzun, *Berlioz and His Century*, 120–29.
15. Berlioz in Piero Weiss and Richard Taruskin, *Music in the Western World: A History in Documents* (New York: Schirmer, 1984), 349.
16. Said probably cites this translation of Berlioz's letter from page 8 of the liner notes of a record: Hector Berlioz, *Les Troyens*, conducted by Colin Davis, Philips 6709 002, 1970, 33⅓ rpm. A different English translation of this letter is published in David Cairns, *Berlioz*, vol. 2, *Servitude and Greatness, 1832–1869* (London: Allen Lane, 1999), 617.
17. See note 16; Cairns, *Berlioz*, 624.
18. Pierre Boulez, "Berlioz and the Realm of the Imaginary," in *Orientations*, 212–19.
19. Herbert Lindenberger, *Historical Drama: The Relation of Literature and Reality* (Chicago: University of Chicago Press, 1975), 62.
20. Rushton, "Overture to *Les Troyens*," 120.
21. Said refers to the following statement: "The conquest of the earth, which mostly means the taking it away from those who have a different complexion or slightly flatter noses than ourselves, is not a pretty thing when you look into it too much." Joseph Conrad, *Heart of Darkness and the Secret Sharer* (New York: New American Library, 1950), 69.
22. Alexis de Tocqueville in Jean Martin, *L'empire renaissant: 1789–1871* (Paris: Denoël, 1987), 305–6. The translation from the French is Said's.

4. CREATION AND COHERENCE IN *DIE MEISTERSINGER*

1. Dieter Borchmeyer, "The Question of Anti-Semitism," in *Wagner Handbook*, ed. Ulrich Müller and Peter Wapnewski, trans. John Deathridge (Cambridge, Mass.: Harvard University Press), 166–85.
2. Edward Said, "The Importance of Being Unfaithful to Wagner," *London Review of Books*, February 11, 1993, 11–12.
3. Theodor W. Adorno, *In Search of Wagner*, trans. Rodney Livingstone (London: New Left, 1981).

4. Paul Lawrence Rose, *Wagner: Race and Revolution* (New Haven, Conn.: Yale University Press, 1992), 189–92.
5. Hans Rudolf Vaget, "Sixtus Beckmesser—a 'Jew in the Brambles?'," *Opera Quarterly* 12, no. 1 (1995): 35–45; Adorno, *In Search of Wagner*, 21–27; Barry Millington, "Nuremberg Trial: Is There Anti-Semitism in *Die Meistersinger*?," *Cambridge Opera Journal* 3, no. 3 (1991): 247–60.
6. Vaget, "Sixtus Beckmesser," 43.
7. Robert Donington, *Opera and Its Symbols: The Unity of Words, Music, and Staging* (New Haven, Conn.: Yale University Press, 1990), 95–140; Deryck Cooke, *I Saw the World End: A Study of Wagner's Ring* (New York: Oxford University Press, 1979).
8. Marc A. Weiner, *Richard Wagner and the Anti-Semitic Imagination* (Lincoln: University of Nebraska Press, 1995).
9. Thomas Grey, "Bodies of Evidence," *Cambridge Opera Journal* 8, no. 2 (1996): 185–97.
10. Theodor W. Adorno, "Wagners Aktualität," in *Gesammelte Schriften*, ed. Rolf Tiedemann, vol. 16 (Frankfurt: Suhrkamp, 1978), 543–64; an English translation by Susan Gillespie was published as "Wagner's Relevance for Today," *Grand Street*, no. 44 (1993): 32–59.
11. Adorno, "Wagner's Relevance for Today," 35; Pierre Boulez, *Orientations: Collected Writings*, ed. Jean-Jacques Nattiez (Cambridge, Mass.: Harvard University Press, 1986), 223–30.
12. Adorno, 37. The additions between square brackets are Said's.
13. Adorno, 40.
14. Adorno, 45.
15. Hegel quoted in Adorno, 41. Adorno quotes from the first volume of G. W. F. Hegel's *Vorlesungen über die Philosophie der Geschichte* (1837).
16. Adorno, "Wagner's Relevance for Today," 47.
17. John Warrack, *Richard Wagner: Die Meistersinger von Nürnberg* (Cambridge: Cambridge University Press, 1994), 19–24.
18. Edward T. Cone, "The World of Opera and Its Inhabitants," in *Music: A View from Delft: Selected Essays*, ed. Robert P. Morgan (Chicago: University of Chicago Press, 1989), 130.
19. There is a very fine study of Wagner's proleptic and typological methods in the construction of his emblematic city: Arthur Groos, "Constructing Nuremberg: Typological and Proleptic Communities in *Die Meistersinger*," *Nineteenth-Century Music* 16, no. 1 (1992): 19–34 (Edward Said's note).
20. Weiner, *Richard Wagner and the Anti-Semitic Imagination*, 215–16.

21. Weiner, 217.
22. George Eliot, *Middlemarch: An Authoritative Text, Background, Reviews, and Criticism*, ed. Bert G. Hornback (New York: Norton, 1977), xiii.
23. Eliot, 200.
24. Eliot, 64.
25. Eliot, 64.
26. Friedrich Nietzsche, *The Birth of Tragedy and The Case of Wagner*, trans. Walter Kaufmann (New York: Vintage, 1967), 76–86.
27. Adorno, "Wagner's Relevance for Today," 54–55.
28. Martin Gregor-Dellin and Dietrich Mack, ed., *Cosima Wagner's Diaries*, trans. Geoffrey Skelton, vol. 1, *1869–1877* (New York: Harcourt Brace Jovanovich, 1978), 121, 232, 336.
29. Charles Rosen, *The Romantic Generation* (Cambridge, Mass.: Harvard University Press, 1995).
30. Adorno, *In Search of Wagner*, 45–47.
31. Carl Dahlhaus, *Richard Wagner's Music Dramas*, trans. Mary Whittall (Cambridge: Cambridge University Press, 1979), 69.
32. Dahlhaus, *Richard Wagner's Music Dramas*, 72–73.

INDEX